THE *MONA LISA* VANISHES

THE MONA LISA VANISHES

A LEGENDARY PAINTER, A SHOCKING HEIST, AND THE BIRTH OF A GLOBAL CELEBRITY

NICHOLAS DAY

WITH ART BY
BRETT HELQUIST

RANDOM HOUSE STUDIO
NEW YORK

All rights reserved. Published in the United States by Random House Studio, an imprint of
Random House Children's Books, a division of Penguin Random House LLC, New York.

Random House Studio with colophon is a registered trademark of Penguin Random House LLC.

Visit us on the Web! rhcbooks.com

Educators and librarians, for a variety of teaching tools, visit us at RHTeachersLibrarians.com

Library of Congress Cataloging-in-Publication Data is available upon request.
ISBN 978-0-593-64384-6 (trade)—ISBN 978-0-593-64385-3 (lib. bdg.)—ISBN 978-0-593-64386-0 (ebook)

The artist used oil on paper to create the illustrations for this book.
The text of this book is set in 12.5-point Adobe Garamond Pro.
Interior design by Michelle Crowe
Hand-drawn frames vector art used under license from Shutterstock.com

Printed in the United States of America
10 9 8 7 6 5
First Edition

FOR ISAIAH
—N.D.

FOR FRANCES AND HENRY
—B.H.

CONTENTS

A STAR IS BORN

SHE'S GONE

TELL ME, TELL ME, TELL ME

A STAR IS BORN

IN WHICH THE *MONA LISA* IS PAINTED, IS STOLEN, AND BECOMES AN ABSOLUTE LEGEND

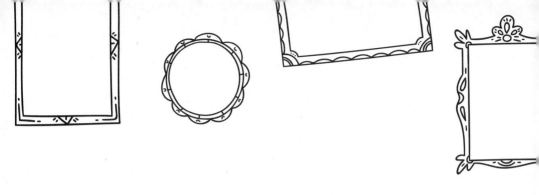

THE CREATION OF THE *MONA LISA*

IMAGINE A PALAZZO—A MAGNIFICENT RENAISSANCE BUILDING.

It's Florence, 1503. There are a lot of palazzos around. Choose a good one.

Now imagine a man: handsome, charming, gentle. Make him a painter.

Imagine a woman: intriguing, unknown, beautiful. Make her a model.

Do you see them?

Neither of them should be there.

The man shouldn't be a painter at all. Born into a long line of notaries—an early version of a lawyer—the man should have gone into the family business. Being a notary may have been the most boring profession in Renaissance Italy, but it was steady.

Instead, he designed flying machines. He dissected dead bodies. He inflated pig bladders and launched them around the

1

room. He was an extraordinary, ingenious, wondrously weird man.

He was Leonardo da Vinci. He painted a little too.

But he didn't have a reason to paint this portrait of an ordinary Florentine woman.

The woman shouldn't be posing for him. She shouldn't be in a room with any man. She should be hidden away in a convent, the home of a Catholic religious order.

Her family hadn't had enough money for a dowry, the sum any girl in Florence needed for a marriage, and girls without dowries disappeared into convents, cut off from the world. But a marriage was arranged, somehow, and she prospered. There were children, and there was money—enough money to commission a painting.

Thanks to that painting, she became the most recognizable face in the world.

We don't know how long she sat for Leonardo. We don't know if they ever saw each other again.

We do know that afterward, the woman staring out of the painting—Lisa Gherardini—will watch as the city around her is invaded and pillaged. It will be brutal. Upon her husband's death, she will finally enter a convent.

We know that the man staring into the painting—Leonardo da Vinci—will flee Florence. He'll move up and down Italy, a brilliant artist without a place to call his own. As an old man, he will end up in another country altogether. When he makes the journey over the Alps to France, he will strap this portrait, the *Mona Lisa,* to a donkey.

He will die.

But what happens in that palazzo will make her ageless. She will live through the centuries.

She will become immortal. She cannot die.

She can, however, be kidnapped.

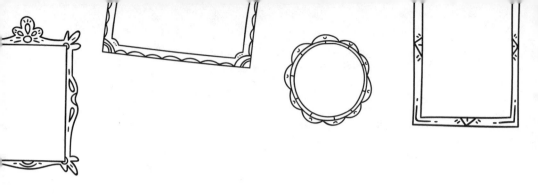

THE THEFT OF THE *MONA LISA*

T WAS MONDAY, AUGUST 21, 1911, AND IT WAS MORNING, FINALLY. FROM HIS hiding place inside the closet, the man could hear the footsteps of the Louvre guards.

In the empty, enormous rooms of the Louvre, the footsteps must have echoed.

They came closer, and closer still, and then—*farther.* Each time, the guards walked right past him. He had no idea if they were looking for him. But they should have been. On Sunday, the man had come to the Louvre just like any other visitor, but when the museum was closing, he didn't do what the other visitors did.

He didn't leave.

The Louvre wasn't a hotel. You weren't supposed to spend the night. But a few months before, a French journalist had done the same thing. The journalist didn't think the Louvre's security was any good, and to prove it, when the museum closed, he crawled inside the sarcophagus of an Egyptian king and stayed there until the morning.

He was right about the security. No one bothered him. Not even the Egyptian king whose sarcophagus he'd borrowed.

All the journalist took from the Louvre was material for an article, an exposé on the museum's lousy security.

This man wanted to take more than that.

THEY'D BOTH GONE UNNOTICED BECAUSE THE LOUVRE WASN'T JUST AN ART museum. It was a labyrinth, with a thousand years of hiding places.

It was first built as a medieval fortress, complete with a moat. It became a palace, the magnificent home of French royalty. With every monarch, the palace grew yet more palatial, sprouting vast wings and pavilions like some sort of fantastical beast. After the French Revolution, which overthrew the monarchy, it completed its final transformation into a museum, a monument for the new French Republic.

By then, it sprawled. It occupied the space of nearly forty football fields. It was as long as the Eiffel Tower if the Eiffel Tower were laid down on the ground and lined up end to end with *another* Eiffel Tower. It was a seemingly endless expanse of grand rooms, like a mirror reflected in a mirror.

Alongside those rooms were centuries of nooks and crannies. These were less grand: storerooms, cupboards, annexes, cubbyholes. A human being could squeeze in almost anywhere. A century ago, no one at the Louvre even knew how many of these hideaways there were. There were too many to count.

And on Monday, August 21, 1911, no one at the Louvre knew that someone was hidden away inside one of them.

This man had rejected the sarcophagus in favor of a storage closet. The Louvre was also a sort of art studio, where amateurs came to copy the paintings of the greats. The museum let these copyists—that was the term for them—store their things there.

When the Louvre closed on Sunday, the man slipped in among the easels and paint boxes.

That was the easy part. What came next was harder.

The man waited behind the closet door. He listened to the footsteps.

***

LET US LEAVE HIM THERE FOR A MINUTE.

He's completely still, but outside the museum, a new century is accelerating. Everything is in motion.

The changes have been blindingly fast. New inventions like automobiles and airplanes are a blur on the street and in the sky. Their speed is altering fundamental facts of life—things as basic as *time* and *space*. People can move across the globe at unimagined velocity, connecting places that were once isolated. Information follows at the same breathtaking pace. All of this is shrinking the world. A local story—the story of a criminal at loose in the Louvre, for example—can now become a global sensation.

All of this will shape what happens when the closet door opens.

It will be a story at the mercy of this new breakneck century.

⌒

THE HALLS OF THE LOUVRE WENT QUIET.

A closet door cracked.

When the man stepped out of the storage closet—sleepless from a night with the easels, sweaty in the August heat—he was alone.

Or almost alone. He was surrounded by the most extraordinary paintings in the world.

The storage closet had an extremely good location—a suspiciously good location. Around the corner was the Salon Carré, the home of the most prized paintings in the Louvre. The great Italian painters were all represented: Raphael, Titian, Tintoretto. And Leonardo da Vinci.

The museum was closed on Mondays, but it wasn't abandoned. The staff still came in: curators, cleaners, maintenance workers. There were guards too, but fewer, and they had to cover an area the size of a small city.

None of them saw the man leave the closet. But if any had,

they might not have noticed. He was wearing a white smock, the uniform of the Louvre maintenance workers. It was a suit of invisibility. He was too normal to be noticed.

He didn't look like a thief.

He walked around the corner into the Salon Carré, the heart of the Louvre. It was all his for the taking.

The paintings in the Louvre were not locked down. This lack of security was actually a form of security: in case of fire, the guards were supposed to grab the paintings and run. Still, some paintings—especially valuable paintings—were hung in a way that required inside knowledge. They had to be removed from their hooks in a very precise way, a way that anyone who didn't already know was unlikely to figure out fast.

The painting the man wanted was hung that way.

Luckily, he didn't have to figure it out. He already knew. He slid it off the hooks in seconds.

It was all going according to plan.

On the wall, the painting was sublime. Off the wall, it was agony. Painted not on canvas but on wood, surrounded by an antique frame and glass, the whole thing weighed in at almost two hundred pounds.

Somehow, the man wrestled it into the nearest stairwell. Here, he was safe—or safer. He removed the glass case and cut away the frame. The painting itself was all that was left: three slabs of wood joined together, measuring less than three feet high and two feet wide.

It was over four hundred years old. And it was his.

Almost.

There was a problem. A painting on canvas, once outside of its frame, can be rolled up. A painting on wood can never be rolled up. A slab of wood is always the size of the slab of wood.

There was no good solution. So he went with a bad solution: he put the painting—fragile, irreplaceable, unprotected—under his sweaty white smock.

He started down the stairwell, and when he reached the bottom, he opened the door—or he *tried* to open the door. The door was locked. He put its key in the lock and opened the door—or he *tried* to open the door. The key didn't work.

Suddenly, it was not all going according to plan.

The man removed the doorknob with a screwdriver. But removing a doorknob doesn't open a locked door—the door is still locked—and before he could do anything else, he heard footsteps. Someone, possibly a guard—probably a guard—was coming down the stairs.

He was trapped. He was cornered at the bottom of a stairwell, sweaty and sleepless, with a priceless painting poorly hidden under his smock. It wasn't a good look.

The footsteps came closer, and closer, and then . . .

It wasn't a guard. It was a plumber. The Louvre was so large it had its own plumbers.

The plumber saw a man at the bottom of the stairwell. Who did he see? What did he see? Did he see the sweat? Did he see the desperation? Did he see the shape of a painting?

The man at the bottom spoke first. He didn't make excuses. He didn't explain what he was doing there. He acted like he belonged. *Look at this door,* he said to the plumber. *It doesn't even have a doorknob! How am I supposed to get out of here?*

The plumber saw the white smock. He saw someone too normal to be noticed. With his pliers, the plumber twisted the inner workings of the lock. It sprang open, and the man sprang out of the trap. He walked out of the stairwell, into a courtyard, through a gallery, and toward the Louvre's entrance.

There was a guard at the entrance—or there was supposed to be a guard at the entrance. But at this minute, on this Monday morning, the guard was gone. He was fetching a bucket of water.

He'd picked the worst time in the long history of the Louvre to clean his booth.

The man in the white smock—sweaty, sleepless, triumphant—walked out of the Louvre and into Paris.

Then he disappeared.

He'd stolen two things from the Louvre.

The first was a doorknob.

No one would care about the doorknob.

The second was the *Mona Lisa*.

A lot of people would care a lot about the *Mona Lisa*.

THE LUDICROUS FAME OF THE *MONA LISA*

THE THEFT OF THE *MONA LISA* WAS THE GREATEST HEIST IN ART HISTORY. Every heist that followed—every stolen painting—was an imitation.

Not an imitation of the strategy, or the craft, or the luck, but an imitation of the sheer bravado: the idea of stealing something that *couldn't possibly be stolen.*

A year before the theft, in a spooky coincidence, the director of the Louvre had been asked about the possibility: Could the *Mona Lisa* be stolen? The director had laughed. He'd said the *Mona Lisa* would be no easier to steal than the massive towers of Notre-Dame, the medieval French cathedral.

It was a question that didn't interest many people. Before the *Mona Lisa* was stolen, most people had never heard of it. Outside of select circles—artists, art lovers, people lost in the Louvre—the painting hardly existed. It was just another work by Leonardo da Vinci. A strange, small, dark portrait.

After it was stolen, it became a sensation.

For the *Mona Lisa,* being stolen was a very good career move.

Today, the painting is so famous that stealing it sounds like a joke. It sounds like stealing the Washington Monument or Niagara Falls; it sounds absurd. The *Mona Lisa* is so popular today it can hardly be seen: a visitor to the Louvre is lucky to get close enough to catch a glimpse, to confirm that it exists. But that's enough, because every visitor to the Louvre already knows what the *Mona Lisa* is supposed to look like.

The reason they know is because of what happened on August 21, 1911.

Before that date, it was possible to see the *Mona Lisa* without already knowing what the *Mona Lisa* looks like.

Afterward, it was not.

This is a story about how a strange, small portrait became the most famous painting in history. It's about a shocking theft and a bizarre recovery. It's a glimpse of a new age—a future of conspiracy theories and instant celebrity.

But it is also the story of another way of looking at the world—clearly, plainly, without assumptions or expectations. It's the story of how Leonardo da Vinci looked at the world.

To solve the theft of Leonardo's painting, the world needed someone like Leonardo da Vinci himself: someone who *observes.*

The world would not get Leonardo.

Like the *Mona Lisa* that August in Paris, Leonardo was long gone.

SHE'S GONE

IN WHICH NO ONE NOTICES THAT THE *MONA LISA* IS MISSING, AND THEN EVERYONE EVERYWHERE NOTICES

MONDAY MORNING

FOR A MOMENT—JUST A MOMENT—PUT THE MAN IN THE WHITE SMOCK back in his closet.

Make him sleepless and sweaty again. Make him not yet triumphant.

Bring back the footsteps.

The footsteps were from a crew of workmen—the men who were supposed to be in white smocks. They walked toward the Salon Carré, where the head of the crew—the head of all maintenance at the Louvre—stopped his men. "This," he said, pointing to the *Mona Lisa,* "is the most valuable painting in the world." He used the French name for the painting: *La Joconde.*

The crew looked at the *Mona Lisa.* They had no idea that they were the last people who would see it in the Louvre for a very long time.

After they left, the man came out of the closet. He went into the Salon Carré; he went out of the Salon Carré; he went down a stairwell.

At which point, the same workmen walked back through the Salon Carré. It was only an hour after they'd been there before, but something had changed, and they saw it immediately. Or, rather, they *didn't* see it.

They didn't see the *Mona Lisa*. They saw a blank space on the wall and some iron hooks.

It was a pivotal moment. The painting had been gone less than an hour, maybe even less than a few minutes. Time was precious. The thief might have still been in the Louvre.

The crew stared at the wall, dumbfounded.

Finally, the head of the crew said, "They have taken it away for fear we would steal it."

He laughed. Everyone laughed.

The logic was simple. The *Mona Lisa* couldn't be stolen. The director of the Louvre had said so himself. If it *couldn't* be stolen, that meant it *wasn't* stolen. So if it was gone—and it *was* gone—that must mean it was even more secure than usual.

Problem solved.

The workmen walked out of the Salon Carré. They told no one about the blank wall. They didn't think twice about it.

The moment passed.

The *Mona Lisa* had been stolen—and no one knew it.

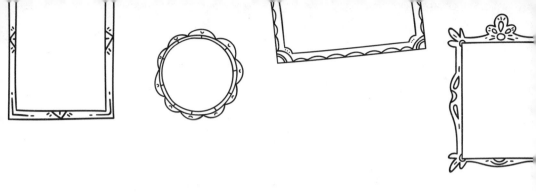

BRIGADIER PAUPARDIN HAS A VERY BAD DAY

BRIGADIER MAXIMILIEN ALPHONSE PAUPARDIN DEFINITELY DID NOT know it.

This was unfortunate, because Brigadier Paupardin was the guard in charge of the Salon Carré. His whole job—his only job—was to know if a painting was stolen.

On Tuesday morning, twenty-four hours after the *Mona Lisa* left the Louvre, Paupardin showed up to work. Tuesday, August 22, 1911, would have been a good day not to show up for work. It would have been a good day to be sick. It would have been a good day to pretend to be sick. It was not a good day to be a guard at the Louvre, and especially not a guard named Maximilien Alphonse Paupardin.

He was not a good guard, but none of the guards at the Louvre were good guards. Like Paupardin, they were retired French army officers—it was a job requirement—and they were old and tired. They'd taken a job at the Louvre because it was the stuffiest place in Paris. Nothing would happen there, and after nothing happened for long enough, they'd retire.

Nothing would happen because nothing ever happened at the Louvre.

Tuesday was a blisteringly hot day. That August, the highs in Paris hit ninety degrees and then went higher. There was no rain. There was no air-conditioning. No one in Paris was at their best. Paupardin was certainly not at his best when he arrived at his post in the Salon Carré.

Paupardin was a terrible guard, but it would take a guard at a new level of terrible not to notice that a painting was missing. Paupardin was terrible, but not next-level terrible. He noticed.

He wasn't the only one. For over a day—ever since the workmen had left—anyone who'd walked through the Salon Carré had seen that the *Mona Lisa* was missing. It was impossible to walk through the Salon Carré *without* seeing that it was missing. But everyone knew that the *Mona Lisa* couldn't be stolen, and if it couldn't be stolen, then it wasn't stolen.

Besides, if the painting *had* been stolen, surely someone would have said something.

Surely the guards would have said something.

Paupardin said nothing. He asked no questions, pulled no alarms, notified no supervisors. Like everyone else, he found a reason to assume it made sense for the *Mona Lisa* to be missing. His reason was that the Louvre photographers had taken it.

In 1911, photography was still a new technology, but it was improving rapidly, and the Louvre was photographing its entire collection. The official photographers had a studio in the museum, and the run of the place. Without asking anyone, without even telling anyone, they removed paintings from the galleries. They photographed the paintings at their leisure and returned them at their leisure.

So when a well-dressed, middle-aged painter named Louis Béroud asked Brigadier Paupardin where the *Mona Lisa* had gone, the guard knew who to blame.

Being photographed, I suppose, he said.

⌒◞

LOUIS BÉROUD HAD WOKEN UP THAT MORNING WITH AN IDEA.

It was not a new idea—not exactly. Louis Béroud did not value new ideas. He was a conservative man who valued tradition, and he painted traditionally.

Béroud specialized in lovingly detailed depictions of the Louvre. He knew the museum well. He'd spent many days painting there; he'd set many paintings there. In 1911, it was still a quiet place. Visitors and copyists had extraordinary access to the paintings, and they could sit with a work all day almost undisturbed. Béroud was especially fascinated by the copyists of the Louvre. He painted the copyists and their paintings in front of the paintings that *they* were painting—a scene that he himself was painting. It was a Möbius strip of a subject.

Louis Béroud loved the Louvre. But something had come between him and his beloved museum. That something was almost invisible, but it was all Louis Béroud could see.

It was a single pane of glass.

A few years before, a prized painting in the Louvre had been attacked with scissors and sliced through. In response, the museum had decided to put its most valuable works behind glass. The decision was greeted with outrage by critics who said the public would no longer be able to see the paintings—they'd only be able to see themselves reflected in the glass.

Someone brought a razor to the Louvre in protest. He didn't slash a painting.

He shaved his beard.

While reflected in a Rembrandt.

A rumor spread that the *Mona Lisa* had been replaced by a forgery—but behind glass, no one could tell. The real *Mona Lisa,* according to the rumor, belonged to an American millionaire. Asked about the rumor, the director of the Louvre, Théophile Homolle, laughed. That was when he said it would be no easier to steal the *Mona Lisa* than the towers of Notre-Dame.

Louis Béroud despised the glass. He felt it destroyed the intimacy of the Louvre. For Béroud, the glass was a problem, not a solution, and on this Tuesday morning, he was planning a painting that would mock it. He was going to riff on the man who'd shaved in front of a Rembrandt. He would paint a girl in front of the *Mona Lisa,* but in his painting the girl would be arranging her hair in the reflection. We can no longer see the *Mona Lisa,* his painting would say. We can only see ourselves.

Béroud dressed. He did not dress for the heat. He dressed, as he always did, conservatively. He wore black.

When he walked across Paris to the Louvre, through the thick air, the towers of Notre-Dame were still there.

Inside the Louvre, Béroud passed the Grande Galerie—a colossal hallway extending some twelve hundred feet—and headed for the Italian wing. He greeted the guards; he collected his paints and his easel; he entered the Salon Carré.

He entered history.

Louis Béroud had devoted his life to painting. But from this moment on, he will forever be associated with someone else's painting.

He will be Louis Béroud, the man who discovered the *Mona Lisa* was gone.

~

"WHERE IS THE *MONA LISA*?" BÉROUD ASKED.

Being photographed, I suppose, said Brigadier Paupardin.

Béroud sighed. He waited. He left. He returned.

The *Mona Lisa* had not returned. The *Mona Lisa* was taking a very long time to sit for a photograph.

Béroud was getting impatient. He'd planned his day around this painting. He couldn't paint a girl not looking at the *Mona Lisa* without the *Mona Lisa*.

The day is wasted, he told Paupardin. *Do me a favor. Find out when she will return.*

Paupardin left the Salon Carré and walked through the Louvre to the photography studio. He asked where the *Mona Lisa* was. This was when things got extremely confusing. The photographers didn't have the *Mona Lisa*. The photographers hadn't seen the *Mona Lisa*. The photographers had no idea what Paupardin was talking about.

This was not the right answer—this was an extremely wrong answer—so Paupardin repeated the question.

He got the same answer.

Paupardin searched the studio himself. The *Mona Lisa* was not there. The *Mona Lisa* was—suddenly, shockingly, impossibly—nowhere.

Even in the August heat, Brigadier Paupardin must have been cold with sweat. If the *Mona Lisa* was missing, then he was responsible. He was the guard of the Salon Carré. He'd spent all morning guarding a room that had *already been robbed*.

He couldn't search the Louvre himself—it was too big. He couldn't even tell the director of the Louvre, because the director himself was missing. (He hadn't been stolen. He was in Mexico.) Paupardin ran to the person unfortunate enough to now be in charge—the curator of Egyptian antiquities, a man named Georges Bénédite.

Paupardin told Bénédite: *"La Joconde, c'est partie!"*

The Mona Lisa, *it is gone!*

It took a while for Bénédite to understand—Paupardin hardly understood himself what he was saying—but when Bénédite understood, he wasn't especially concerned.

After all, the *Mona Lisa* was in no greater danger than the towers of Notre-Dame. Were the towers of Notre-Dame still there? They were. Therefore, the *Mona Lisa* was in the Louvre.

It *had* to be in the Louvre.

Bénédite, Paupardin, and the head of the Louvre guards checked the photography studio again; they checked the Salon Carré.

The *Mona Lisa* was not in the Louvre. They could repeat

"The *Mona Lisa* has to be in the Louvre" as many times as they wanted, but they couldn't make it true.

Phone lines were not private in 1911, and security was essential, so Georges Bénédite didn't call the police. On that brutally hot Tuesday, he walked from the Louvre to the Palais de Justice, the home of the Paris police. It must have been the worst walk of his life.

He had no clues or leads, no evidence or eyewitnesses.

He told the police the only thing did he did know:

"C'est partie."

It is gone.

IT COULD HAVE BEEN WORSE

WAS THE LOUVRE LUCKY?

It's hard to imagine. The dignified French museum was about to be reduced to the status of a laughingstock. *Lucky* doesn't seem like the right word.

But what if Louis Béroud had been less upset about the glass?

What if Louis Béroud had decided it was too hot to walk to the Louvre?

What if Louis Béroud had given up after he found the *Mona Lisa* missing?

The *Mona Lisa* was gone for over twenty-four hours before anyone realized it was gone. If not for the persistence of Louis Béroud, it might have been days. It might have been a week.

The theft of the *Mona Lisa*—the art heist of the century— was discovered because Louis Béroud got bored.

The Louvre was lucky.

In the months and years to come, the Louvre's luck would run out.

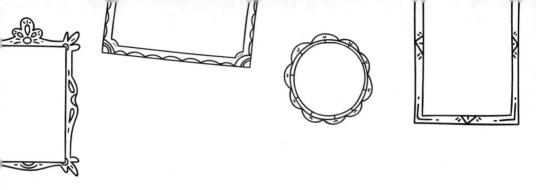

LOUIS LÉPINE IS ON THE CASE

ALMOST AS SOON AS GEORGES BÉNÉDITE ARRIVED AT THE PALAIS DE JUStice, Louis Lépine left for the Louvre.

Only those who already knew him would have noticed him enter. Louis Lépine never made an impression. He was short and slight, and his bowler hat, strangely, made him seem even smaller. He had a kindly white beard that made it look as if a small arctic animal had attached itself to his chin.

But his eyes were sharp and intense, and there was never a question about who would lead the *Mona Lisa* investigation: Louis Lépine was the chief of police in Paris, and he led everything. He led the Paris fire department; he led the French army stationed in

Paris. He was appointed by the president of France, and only the president of France could fire him. A legend in his own time, he was the sort of man who acquired multiple nicknames: the Pooh-Bah of Paris, the Little Man with a Big Stick, the Little King.

He had complete faith in himself. He once decreed that no man *taller* than five feet seven could be a detective in Paris—and that no man *shorter* than five feet nine could be a constable, a street officer. (Applicants who measured five feet eight exactly were never heard from again.) Lépine's theory was that detectives should be inconspicuous, and police officers who walked the street should be conspicuous. It was an idea that was both sensible and utterly senseless.

But Lépine believed it. He was never less than self-confident, and he had reason to be. He'd once saved the French government itself: in the 1890s, he'd achieved national fame for calming widespread riots that had almost tipped the country into revolution.

Could Louis Lépine find an old plank of wood? He could.

His officers swarmed the Louvre. They locked the doors; they took positions on the roof; they told everyone that the emergency was a broken water pipe. The museum staff was left to wonder why the Paris police were fixing plumbing problems when the Louvre had its own plumbers.

The secrecy was partly because Louis Lépine was sure he was about to find the *Mona Lisa*. It must have been simply misplaced, and there was no point in reporting a theft if you were about to solve it. But the secrecy was also because if the *Mona Lisa had* been stolen, it would cause an uproar. The president of France himself would have to be notified.

Lépine conferred with Bénédite. This was no help. Bénédite didn't even know how long the *Mona Lisa* had been missing. (At this point, no one had talked to the workmen who'd seen it the day before.) Anything was possible. The painting could still be in the Louvre. Or it could be almost anywhere in the world.

Lépine acted with royal scope—he was called the Little King for a reason. He ordered the borders of France sealed. Trains would be stopped and searched; so would ships. In fact, any ship that had left France since Sunday would be searched when it docked. As long as the *Mona Lisa* did not stay on the high seas indefinitely, it would be found.

Meanwhile, the Paris police canvassed the museum for clues. They found nothing until an antique frame and a glass box were discovered in a stairwell near the Salon Carré. Both were in good condition.

The label on the frame read: *La Joconde.*

In the late afternoon, the Louvre came clean. Georges Bénédite stood outside the museum and told the truth. "*La Joconde* is gone," he said. "So far, we have not the slightest clue as to the perpetrator of the crime."

THE VERY, VERY SMALL VICTORY
OF LOUIS BÉROUD

PAUSE HERE, BRIEFLY, AND PUT LOUIS BÉROUD BACK IN BED.

Turn back the clock. Make it Tuesday morning again.
And tell him he has won: The *Mona Lisa* is free! It has escaped from its glass prison. No one can use it as a shaving mirror. No one can arrange their hair in its reflection.

But before Louis Béroud gets too excited, tell him there's a slight complication.

Instead of hundreds of admirers, the *Mona Lisa* now has a very select audience. An *extremely* select audience.

An audience of one.

A thief.

UNIMAGINABLE

WITHIN A DAY, ALL OF PARIS HAD HEARD.

They'd seen it as soon as they stepped outside. Paris was a city of newspapers, and the shocking news was in every hand, on every newsstand, across every front page. The same words, over and over again, in extremely large letters:

INIMAGINABLE

INEXPLICABLE

INCROYABLE

The headline in *Le Petit Parisien* used more ink:

**THE MONA LISA *HAS DISAPPEARED FROM*
THE LOUVRE**

Le Petit Parisien was not *petit,* the French word for "small." It was the highest-circulation newspaper in the world, and the *Mona Lisa* theft was plastered across it.

The story had everything. An *unimaginable* theft. A criminal mastermind—and it had to be a criminal mastermind, because who else could steal a painting that couldn't be stolen? A beautiful woman. A genius. A painting worth a sum too staggering to estimate. It was a Hollywood movie before Hollywood even existed.

Overnight, Paris became a city obsessed with a lady.

Parisians who had never heard of the *Mona Lisa* were suddenly consumed by its disappearance. They went to the Louvre even though the Louvre was closed. (Louis Lépine had ordered it closed.) They thronged the street outside the museum just to be close to where the *Mona Lisa* used to be. The only *Mona Lisa* still there was on postcards. They sold well.

The *Mona Lisa* heist ran on the front page of Parisian newspapers every day for over a month. With each story, the painting grew more significant, the loss more tragic. It was no longer just another painting, or even just another great painting. It was a *transcendent* painting.

Over the next month, it was transformed into a painting that was beloved by all, that spoke to everyone, that moved everyone. In fact, it became less a painting and more an object of worship. It was a myth, a mystery, almost a living being.

"What audacious criminal," asked the magazine *L'Illustration,* "what mystifier, what manic collector, what insane lover, has committed this abduction?"

On a single day, *L'Illustration* received more than five hundred letters claiming to have information about the theft. More than one hundred people were so certain they had crucial knowledge that they came to the paper in person. The magazine offered ten thousand francs for any clues leading to the return of the *Mona Lisa*. The *Paris-Journal* raised the reward to fifty thousand francs. It ran a photo of Notre-Dame with a tower missing and the headline:

COULD THIS HAPPEN TOO?

To Louis Lépine, to Georges Bénédite, to Brigadier Paupardin, to the president of France himself, these stories were a daily reminder of their failures. Anyone involved in the investigation got an update on just how badly they were doing every time they passed a newsstand. Each day, the headlines got more insistent and more outraged.

The painting had escaped, but the story was inescapable.

⌒◦

IT WAS THE PERFECT STORY AT THE PERFECT TIME. WHY? BECAUSE ALL OF A sudden, people could *read*.

For centuries, literacy had been a specialized skill. That was changing fast. More people were going to school; more jobs required reading. The result was a surge in literacy.

The side effect was the golden age of newspapers.

In 1870, over one million newspapers were sold every day in Paris. By the time the *Mona Lisa* was stolen, that number was up to almost six million—in a city of less than three million. The price of a daily paper was half what it once was. Mass media had arrived.

Newly popular, the press went in search of the sort of stories that would attract even more readers. Reporters wanted adventure; they wanted crime; they wanted celebrity. They didn't care if their stories were true. Not especially. They cared if they made good copy.

There was a lot of good copy. The world was in upheaval.

It's hard to imagine today just how fast the world was changing in 1911. But try. Step outside on this August morning in 1911.

Ignore the newspapers shouting *INIMAGINABLE.*

Smell the air instead. It's rank. It's toxic. This smell is actually good, by Parisian standards. A few decades before, there were truly noxious episodes known as "the Great Stinks." Still, in the summer heat, the air smells medieval.

Now look down before—*whoops.* That's horse excrement. (And that's the polite name for it.) It's everywhere, although it, too, is improving. A decade before, a Parisian street was an ankle-deep stream of horse droppings. Horse-drawn carriages are still everywhere, but there are also noisy horseless carriages, an invention so new there's only recently a word for them: *automobiles.* The first airplanes are overhead. The new Paris Métro— the subway—is underground.

Planes in the air and horse manure on the pavement: the past and the future are all mixed up together. It's hard to figure out what the present is like when nothing will hold still long enough to let anyone figure it out. The world is in relentless motion.

Now pick up a copy of that newspaper—but ignore the *Mona Lisa* on the front page. Look at the other stories: murder, scandal, corruption, from all over the world. The globe has shrunk: places that were weeks apart are now days; places that were days apart are now hours. A sort of invisible magic that sends information through the thin air is about to revolutionize the world. It's called *radio*. A different magic trick can now preserve the ghosts of the past. It's called *film*.

Look up—those are streetlights coming on above. Paris is ablaze. It's not just the past and the future that are mixed up. Day and night are now jumbled together too. Electricity—also a sort of invisible magic—has turned Paris into the City of Light.

Walk through the newly bright night to the neighborhood of Montmartre. It's shabby and loud; it might not feel safe. Here, an artist named Pablo Picasso is tearing up the idea of perspective, the geometric rules governing the paintings that hang in the Louvre. A physicist named Albert Einstein has just torn up the physical rules of space and time. In his grimy Montmartre apartment, Picasso is doing something similar on canvas: he's twisted space and time into something he calls *cubism*.

His work is brilliant, and to anyone seeing it for the first time, or even the second or the third, it is totally incomprehensible.

It was a lot like the rest of the world in 1911. Life was governed by things that few people could understand. All the advancements of art and science—electricity, the internal combustion engine, the theory of relativity, cubism—had to be explained, and even *then* they often didn't make sense.

A theft that made no sense fit right in. The *Mona Lisa* being stolen was impossible, but impossible things were happening every day, sometimes before breakfast.

It was all weirdly similar to the time that produced the *Mona Lisa*—a time when the world was reborn.

TELL ME, TELL ME, TELL ME

IN WHICH LEONARDO IS BORN,
LEAVES HOME, LEARNS TO PAINT,
AND SPENDS HIS TIME WONDERING
WHAT THE MOON IS MADE OF

VINCI,
APRIL 15, 1452

EONARDO DA VINCI IS BORN AT THE RIGHT TIME IN THE RIGHT PLACE TO
the wrong parents.

The place is Vinci—a small town on the slopes outside of
Florence, the birthplace of the Renaissance.

The time is April 15, 1452—the height of the Renaissance.
The word means "rebirth" in Italian. The Renaissance is a cultural and scientific reawakening, a time of great possibility and
intensity. It's a rebirth of learning itself.

The time and the place are not the problem.

The parents are Ser Piero di Antonio, a well-off notary, and
Caterina di Meo Lippi, a poor peasant teenager.

They are not married. That is the problem.

Leonardo da Vinci is an illegitimate son. He is what's known
as a bastard, a child born out of wedlock. He is Ser Piero's son,
yes, but officially he is not anyone's son. This matters in very
important ways. He will not inherit his father's land. He will not
inherit his status. He will not inherit his profession.

The Renaissance is not just an age of artists and scholars. It's also a time of great wealth, and notaries like Ser Piero were at the center of it. Notaries dealt with contracts and wills, and they kept a tiny fraction of the riches they recorded.

It is a good, secure profession.

But an illegitimate son can never become a legitimate notary. Leonardo is out of a job as soon as he's born. Thanks to this cruel logic, Leonardo da Vinci escapes—barely—a dull alternate existence as a notary.

He cannot stay with his mother either. Orphaned, vulnerable, desperately poor, Caterina can barely support herself. She's utterly powerless and far below Ser Piero in Renaissance society— so far below that Ser Piero never gives a thought to marrying her. She is a peasant; he is a notary. Such marriages do not happen. (In fact, instead of marrying her, Ser Piero arranges a marriage with another peasant *for* her.)

Caterina is the hole in Leonardo's life. She disappears from the historical record so completely that her very identity will be a mystery for centuries. Leonardo's mother and Lisa Gherardini— the future *Mona Lisa*—are at the center of this story, yet we know very little about either. This isn't an accident. In the very male Italian Renaissance, the life of any woman is described in the barest terms: the date of her birth and her marriage, the dates she gave birth to children, and then, finally, the date of her death. Her joys and sorrows, the fabric of her days, are all missing. It is a tragic absence.

Renaissance Italy does not shun illegitimate children. As a young boy, Leonardo is welcomed into Ser Piero's household and raised, among his many legitimate siblings, by his grandparents.

But he never fully belongs. He is always on the outside. This is a peculiar advantage. As an outsider, he learns to see the world more clearly, because he can't afford the luxuries of assumptions or illusions. He has to see the world as it is.

He will have to make his own way through it.

FLORENCE,
1466

NOW BARELY A TEENAGER, LEONARDO HAS GROWN UP AMONG OLIVE groves and vineyards. He's a country boy.

But he has to leave home to seek his fortune—there's nothing for him in Vinci. He cannot be a notary, but he already shows a talent for drawing, and Andrea del Verrocchio, a Florentine painter and sculptor, has agreed to take him on as an apprentice. Leonardo will work for Verrocchio, collaborating on the paintings and sculptures that come out of his studio, and in return he will be taught the foundations of the craft. It is a common arrangement.

What happens later is less common.

LEONARDO ARRIVES IN FLORENCE TO FIND A CITY TURNED INSIDE OUT.

No one knows quite what this strange era is. They do not call it a Renaissance yet; no one at the time knows that there is a rebirth of anything, or what's being reborn. The old ways are gone, but the new ways—the rules that this society will obey—have yet to arrive. In the meantime, anything is possible, or at least anything *might* be possible. The sum of worldly knowledge is expanding daily; fortunes are rising to dizzying heights. But all of this is fragile. An invading army might show up at the city walls without notice, and invading armies, although interested in fortunes, care little for worldly knowledge.

Florence is the ideal place for a young man in a hurry. But Leonardo da Vinci is an unusual young man. He's not in a hurry to acquire a fortune. He's not in a hurry to acquire power. He's in a hurry to acquire knowledge—he wants to know everything that might be possible, and more than a few things that might not be.

First, however, he has to learn how to paint.

This turns out not to be a problem.

By imitating del Verrocchio, by immersing himself in the busy life of the workshop, Leonardo learns how to paint—and then *reinvents* how to paint. He creates a technique called *sfumato,* which comes from the Italian word *fumo,* or "smoke." It's a way of painting that hides the act of painting. The people and things in Leonardo's paintings have no edges, because Leonardo doesn't outline anything. Edges make paintings look *painted.* Leonardo recognizes this. His new technique of sfumato blurs everything together, the way smoke dissolves into air.

So nothing ends in Leonardo's paintings. Nothing really begins either. It all just *blends.*

He can only do this with oil paints. When Leonardo is an apprentice, painters in Italy use tempera: water plus color plus egg yolk. A working art studio keeps chickens. But oil paints have just appeared on the horizon, and Leonardo immediately sees their potential. With oils, layers of paint can be built up to achieve an entirely new effect. They also allow for slow, painstaking work: With oils, an artist can take as long as he wants. He can take forever if need be.

Leonardo frequently needs to take forever. And a day.

⌒⌒

A STORY:

After years as an apprentice, Leonardo collaborates with Verrocchio on a painting, *The Baptism of Christ*. He is assigned, among other elements, an angel. It is not supposed to be the focus of the painting, but it becomes the focus. When Leonardo is done, the angel radiates life. It feels a moment away from turning toward the viewer, like it is about to pop out of the painting. Its curls dance. It hardly seems to have been painted at all.

When Verrocchio sees what Leonardo has done, he puts down his own brush. He never completes a painting again.

Another story:

Around this same time, Ser Piero, Leonardo's father, brings him a wooden shield. It's a commission—someone in Vinci wants the shield painted. Ser Piero has found paying work for his son.

But Leonardo does not treat it as an opportunity to make money. He treats it as an opportunity to be extremely Leonardo. He brings a fantastical monster to life on the shield. Like a witch, he uses bits of actual creatures: bats, grasshoppers, snakes.

He sticks their various dissected parts on the shield. The stink almost drives him out of the room.

Before Ser Piero comes back to collect the shield, Leonardo positions it so that a shaft of sunlight hits it square—and when Ser Piero walks into the room, he sees a monster rise up before his eyes. He nearly faints.

Ser Piero recovers. He buys a different shield for his client in Vinci. He sells Leonardo's monster for a huge profit.

Leonardo likely does not see the profit. He has other things on his mind. They do not involve money. They rarely do.

Get the measurement of the sun.

Observe the goose's foot.

Observe the curling motion of the water, how like it is to hair.

Get the master of arithmetic to show you how to square a triangle.

Describe what sneezing is, what yawning is.

This is what Leonardo has on his mind. These entries are from Leonardo's notebooks, which he begins as a young man and continues for the rest of his life. They are an obsessive record of his thoughts. He crowds each page with questions, drawings, facts, observations, jokes—a portrait of a mind on fire.

There are many lists of things he needs to know, because there are many things he needs to know:

Inflate the lungs of a pig and observe whether they increase
*   in width and in length, or only in width.*
Anatomize the bat.
By what means they walk on ice in Flanders.
The moon is dense; anything heavy is dense; what is the
*   nature of the moon?*

He doesn't need to know these things for anything in particular. He certainly doesn't need them for his paintings. He needs to know them because, well, he needs to know them.

When Leonardo tests out a new quill for writing, he scribbles the same word: *"Dimmi. Dimmi. Dimmi."*

Tell me. Tell me. Tell me.

For Leonardo, the world is a Russian nesting doll: you open it up and there's another doll inside, and inside that doll is *another* doll, and inside that doll, still another doll—there are dolls all the way down. This is how Leonardo's mind works. Each new thought, each new observation, leads to another, which opens up another, which leads . . .

Dimmi. Dimmi. Dimmi.

Leonardo is later—some five hundred years later—called the most relentlessly curious man in history. This has its disadvantages.

He is horrible at finishing anything, because once he gets interested in something else, he loses interest in what he's been doing. Completing something—a painting, a sculpture, an engineering project—means less to him than starting it.

He's never had a proper education; he's never learned Latin, the language of scholarship. He tries to master it. Like a schoolboy, he fills his notebooks with Latin words, but he never really succeeds. He describes himself as an *uomo senza lettere*—an unlettered man.

For Leonardo, this is a boast. It means he sees the world without being blinded by what he thinks it is already going to be. He doesn't have assumptions about what something is or what it means. He doesn't leap to conclusions. His highest values are observation and experience, which is why his notebooks are filled with entries like:

Describe the tongue of a woodpecker.

It's a good way to live.

It's not a good way to get a lot of painting done.

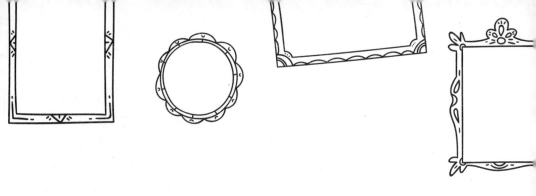

FLORENCE, 1479

WHEN LEONARDO DA VINCI IS BARELY OUT OF HIS APPRENTICESHIP, IT IS already clear that he's not an ordinary artist.

He's not an extraordinary artist either. He's something else altogether.

He does have extraordinary technical abilities—remember that hair on the angel in *The Baptism of Christ,* the painting that caused Verrocchio to abandon painting. Leonardo can paint like an angel. He could open his own studio and make a comfortable living.

But there's more in him than that. The constant scribbling in the notebooks. The drive to know seemingly everything. The questions.

Everyone in Florence can see it. Everyone in Florence knows Leonardo.

He cuts a figure. He wears rose-pink robes that billow behind him. His coats are lined with fur. He sweeps through the streets with an entourage of admirers.

Also, he's beautiful. Everyone agrees about this. Not handsome. Beautiful. His hair falls in long golden locks, like Rapunzel's, cascading down to the middle of his chest. He is tall, and taut with muscle. His early biographers describe him as so strong he can bend the iron ring of a horseshoe. He looks like the Vitruvian Man, whom he would later draw—the perfectly proportional human whose outstretched limbs all touch the sides of a circle. But he's more than physically striking. He is graceful and generous, effortlessly charming, an aid to any party. He has few possessions but collects friends wherever he goes.

The anecdotes go on and on.

But is this true? Or is it too good to be true?

Descriptions of Leonardo read like descriptions of a mythical creature. Each account amplifies the legend: the creature gets more impressive, more fantastic—and harder to believe. But Leonardo's biographers, including those who knew him, all hit the same notes. Their accounts converge. He isn't too good to be true. He is just good enough to be true. He's incredible but real—a narwhal, not a unicorn.

Besides, it isn't that Leonardo is flawless. He has plenty of flaws. His rivals—he will have many—will say he is nothing *but* flaws. They will say he's a pretty boy who can't deliver the goods. Decades later, the great Michelangelo runs into Leonardo in Florence and basically says exactly that.

Michelangelo is a jerk. (History's consensus is that Michelangelo was a jerk.) But he's not entirely wrong.

Sometimes Leonardo can't deliver the goods.

It starts with his very first commission.

Soon after leaving his apprenticeship, Leonardo receives an

invitation to paint an altarpiece in a chapel of the Palazzo Vecchio, Florence's town hall. It is a good commission, an honor. It pays well.

There's an eerie coincidence at work here. At the same time Leonardo receives this commission, a baby girl is born a short walk away. She is baptized Lisa Gherardini.

She will become the *Mona Lisa*. She will change Leonardo's life.

Leonardo could have passed her, swaddled in white linen, on the street. If this were the sort of story that believed in eerie coincidences, we might say that the birth of Lisa Gherardini distracts Leonardo from his altarpiece. That it sends some sort of shudder through the air. That his future flashes before him.

But this story doesn't need eerie coincidences: Leonardo is more than capable of distracting himself.

He starts the altarpiece—and then he gets distracted. The priests of the chapel of the Palazzo Vecchio never get their painting. It's extremely Leonardo to abandon the first commission he ever receives.

Lisa Gherardini will never get her portrait either.

THE *MONA LISA* IS NOWHERE, THE *MONA LISA* IS EVERYWHERE

IN WHICH THE *MONA LISA* REFUSES TO SHOW HER FACE AND THE NEW SCIENCE OF POLICING GOES ON TRIAL

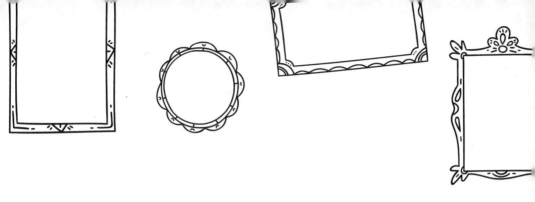

A FEW VERY
SENSIBLE THEORIES

I N THE DAYS AFTER THE THEFT, EVERYONE IN PARIS KNEW WHO HAD STOLEN
the *Mona Lisa*.

Or at least everyone was pretty sure who had stolen the *Mona Lisa*. Or at least everyone was pretty sure they probably knew who had stolen the *Mona Lisa*. Or at least everyone . . .

Paris was a city of wild, untethered rumors.

"Feeling here about the affair is intense," the *New York Times* reported. "An extraordinary number of absurd theories are advanced."

Everyone in Paris could tell you it was obvious what had happened. It was just that everyone told you something different was obvious.

It was blackmail, obviously.

It was sabotage, obviously.

It was the work of a madman, obviously.

It was the work of an extremely wealthy man, obviously.

It was the work of the German government (because Germany and France were close to war over the French colony of Morocco).

It was the work of the French government itself (to distract the public from the fact that Germany and France were close to war).

It was the work of the Louvre itself.

It was the work of a rogue Louvre employee who'd hidden the painting in the museum.

It was the work of a German man who'd been seen in front of the Louvre on Monday, eating peanuts. (Suspicious!)

It was the work of a couple of young German artists who'd been recently seen *in* the Louvre. (Doubly suspicious!)

It was carried out by a man—a man described as *greatly agitated*—who'd boarded a train with something under a horse blanket.

It was carried out by a man—a man described as *in a hurry*—who'd asked an antique shop if they'd be interested in a portrait of an old woman.

It was carried out by no one. The whole thing was a massive hoax.

Newspapers asked fortune-tellers, or clairvoyants, where the painting was. The involvement of fortune-tellers was not a promising sign for the investigation.

They definitively established that the painting was in New York, or London, or in the South of France, hanging in the home of the owner of a soda factory.

One clairvoyant said the painting had been stolen by a birdman—a person *with a neck like an ostrich and hair like feathers.* Still another clairvoyant asked his dog, Pilu, about the *Mona Lisa.* According to Pilu, the painting was still in Paris.

Someone who was not a dog or a clairvoyant told the police the painting was on the steamship *La Champagne,* headed for South America. (Ship searched, no *Mona Lisa.*)

Another person said it was on a freight train in Belgium, headed to a safe house in the Netherlands. (Train searched, no *Mona Lisa.*)

Yet another said it was on the German ocean liner the SS *Kaiser Wilhelm II,* headed to New York: the Germans had stolen the *Mona Lisa* and put it on a ship named after their emperor—the very emperor whose ships were threatening the French off Morocco. It was an outrage; it was an act of war; it was . . .

The *Kaiser Wilhelm II* was searched. There was no *Mona Lisa.*

Thousands of readers wrote to the newspapers with their theories: The painting was in Russia. It was in the United States. It was in Germany, Argentina, Japan, Brazil, Peru, Poland. It was everywhere. It was nowhere. It was maddening.

"Are we dealing with a real theft," asked the *Paris-Journal,* "or a practical joke?"

"This surpasses the imagination," *Le Figaro* complained. "One is tempted to laugh about it as though it were a bad joke. But soon one becomes angry."

It was around this time that some French musicians working

in a casino on the coast took a break from their set. They went for a swim. While in the water, they found a bottle floating alongside them. There was a message in the bottle.

The *Mona Lisa*, the message read, had been tossed into the sea and would never be seen again.

Even in the ocean, a person could not escape the *Mona Lisa*.

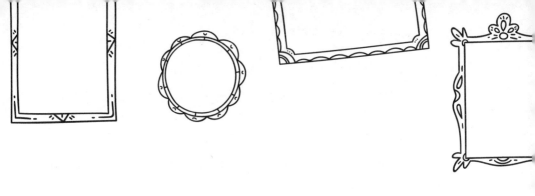

THE LOUVRE IS A CRIME SCENE

THE PARIS POLICE HAD RECENTLY GOTTEN A NEW JOB: SOLVING CRIMES.
For centuries, the police hadn't been in this business. In France and elsewhere, their job was to keep order—to make sure things stayed quiet and to make sure things didn't change. When they did solve crimes, it was often by accident. Investigations were as likely to finger the innocent as the guilty.

But this new century was the dawn of what was optimistically called *forensic science.* It was a fancy way of saying that the police were beginning to figure out how to do police work. This was in part thanks to Louis Lépine. He'd reformed the Paris police, introducing professional standards to a scattershot operation. Investigations would now be carried out with rigor instead of just feel. They'd be scientific—hence, forensic *science.*

That was the idea, anyway. The reality was more complicated. The reality was less scientific.

In the search for the *Mona Lisa,* Louis Lépine was partnered with Alphonse Bertillon, a pioneer in this new field of forensic science. It was a superhero duo of early criminology. There weren't two people in the world who were better at cracking cases.

But they came with their own blind spots.

And soon, those blind spots would make it hard to see what they were looking for.

⌒

TUESDAY—THE DAY AFTER THE THEFT—PASSED. WEDNESDAY. THURSDAY. Friday.

No tourists went inside the Louvre. No copyists, no aspiring thieves, no lovestruck Parisian couples. The Louvre was closed. The Louvre was a crime scene.

The Paris police occupied the museum, claiming director Théophile Homolle's office as their headquarters. Homolle wasn't using it, because he was trying to get back from Mexico before he was fired.

He made it back in time. *Then* he was fired.

Homolle wasn't alone. The loss of the *Mona Lisa* was a national embarrassment, and everyone in power was trying to get back to Paris—they'd all fled in the August heat. They were trying to save themselves and maybe the *Mona Lisa* too.

The first task of the investigation was both incredibly easy and incredibly hard: the police had to make sure the *Mona Lisa* was no longer in the Louvre. The museum administration insisted that the painting hadn't left. Surely, someone would have seen a wooden painting walk out of the museum, they said.

Surely. You can almost hear the administration trying to convince themselves: *Surely.*

Every inch of the Louvre was searched: the nooks and crannies, the cupboards, closets, and cubbyholes. It was a massive undertaking.

Remember that the Louvre was longer than the Eiffel Tower laid down next to another Eiffel Tower. The *Mona Lisa* was tiny—the size of the smallest, skinniest tourist at the Eiffel Tower.

If a human being could hide in the Louvre, an object the size of the *Mona Lisa* could vanish.

Parisians stood vigil outside the Louvre. They paid their respects to the departed.

The doors stayed shut.

~~~

A WEIRD THING HAPPENED DURING THE SEARCH FOR THE *MONA LISA*: THE theft became a work of art itself.

When we call anything *art*—whether it is a painting, or a video, or a urinal (an actual thing people have called art)—we are saying, *This is interesting. Look at this.* The word *art* is a way of marking something as worthy of our attention.

And nothing demanded more attention than the disappearance of the *Mona Lisa.*

In the weeks after the theft, every detail of August 21, 1911, was examined. Everything odd, everything ordinary. It was as if the aliens had come down to Earth at last but what they wanted was not our genetic code, or our fresh water, or our electric guitars. What they wanted was to know about August in Paris in 1911. But we had to tell them *everything*.

In the investigation, all the details of that day came out. It was a perfect re-creation of an almost ordinary day.

The investigators discovered that a guard had taken a long bathroom break to smoke a cigarette. That a guard had stayed home because his children had the measles. That a guard at an entrance had taken a nap. They discovered that security was slapdash, paintings were moved without authorization, and the museum photographers ran the place.

The Louvre staff were interviewed. They weren't happy about it. They were already resentful—they'd recently lost a battle to unionize—and some stopped talking to the police. Their silence was suspicious. Unless it was normal. Who knew? That was the problem: no one knew anything, so even normal things were suspicious. The most mundane act, the most average visitor, could be a clue. It was exhilarating and exasperating.

It certainly made it hard to think clearly. When Brigadier Paupardin was interviewed by the police, he mostly remembered the heat. But he had a dim recollection of a frequent visitor to the Salon Carré. This visitor was a young man who was especially interested in the *Mona Lisa*. Maybe only interested in the *Mona Lisa*. Maybe *too* interested in the *Mona Lisa*.

The police were already wondering if the painting had been stolen by a besotted visitor. The *Mona Lisa,* unlike other paintings in the Louvre, got mail. Love letters. Mash notes. Valentines. Just before the theft, a postcard had been sent to the *Mona Lisa,* care of the Louvre. "I love you," the writing on the postcard declared. "I love you. I adore you. I adore you." It went on like this for a while.

In France, a land of love affairs, this explanation—that the *Mona Lisa* was kidnapped by a would-be lover—seemed logical, maybe even inevitable.

The police questioned Paupardin, who said that the *Mona Lisa*'s suitor was quiet and inconspicuous. Indeed, he was an ideal museum visitor. But—and this was the key detail that Paupardin told the police—he was German.

A young man in love with the *Mona Lisa* was suspicious. A German in love with it was *extremely* suspicious.

An all-points bulletin was issued, and the police found someone matching the young German man's description in the south of France. This young man was interrogated—but he hadn't been in Paris on August 21. He hadn't even been near Paris. He was released, and the police were forced to admit that their prime suspect had been someone guilty only of looking at art in an art museum.

They did find a witness who'd seen a man leave the Louvre the morning of the theft. The witness said the man was carrying a rectangular package and that he'd thrown something in a ditch. The ditch was searched, and a doorknob was found—the same doorknob that was missing from the bottom of the stairwell. It seemed like a breakthrough. But the witness knew nothing else. When asked for a description, he described the person as *ordinary*.

The breakthrough had broken through to nothing.

Also, why would the thief get rid of the doorknob where it could be found? He was about to cross over the Seine, the river that runs through Paris. Why not throw the doorknob in the water? It made no sense. Was he that bad of a thief? That was impossible: he'd just stolen the *Mona Lisa*; he *couldn't* be that bad of a thief. Did he throw the doorknob there to distract the investigation? Was it a false lead? Could nothing be trusted?

A week after the theft, the police issued a brief progress report. The investigation had established a couple of facts: First, the *Mona Lisa* was definitely not in the Louvre. And second, the theft was planned and "executed with unequaled audacity."

In a brilliant bit of policing, the investigation had successfully established what everyone already knew.

In Paris, there were a pair of theories:

The police weren't talking because they knew exactly what they were doing.

The police weren't talking because they had no idea what they were doing.

It was entirely possible that both theories were true.

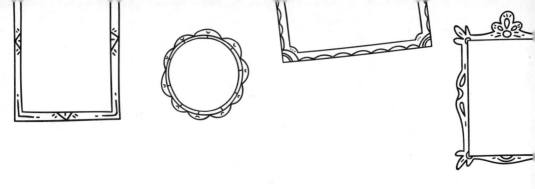

THE MAN WITH THE
WRONG NAME

U NLIKE LOUIS LÉPINE, ALPHONSE BERTILLON, HIS PARTNER IN THE *MONA Lisa* investigation, had zero nicknames.

In fact, he didn't even have his own name.

When Bertillon's father registered the birth of his son, he couldn't remember the name he and his wife had chosen. All he remembered was that it began with an *A*. So he guessed—and he guessed wrong. The man who was supposed to be Albert Bertillon went through life under the name Alphonse.

Alphonse Bertillon, the man with the wrong name, would spend his career trying to find the right names for everyone else. The problem of identification plagued policing. Aliases— fake identities—almost always worked because the police had no good way to keep track of who was who. Until the practice was banned, convicted criminals were literally *branded* as criminals—they were burned with a hot iron, like cattle. It was the only way to guarantee they could be identified after release.

It was a horrible, inhumane system. When Bertillon joined

the Paris police, he was an unlikely candidate to change it. A sarcastic, temperamental man, he'd been expelled from three different schools. (He'd once set fire to his own desk.) He ended up in the identification bureau of the Paris police only because he'd failed everywhere else. It was a dead-end job. The descriptions in the bureau's files were supposed to help identify suspects, but they were comically vague: "Stature: Average. Face: Ordinary." It was barely better than writing down "Man." The work was pointless.

After years of internal resistance, Bertillon converted the Paris police to a new system, which he modestly called the Bertillon system. It called for the police to take a series of incredibly specific measurements—the length of the right ear, for example, or the length of the left middle finger. The nose was split into multiple sections: height, width, projection. With the right measurements, Bertillon believed, someone could be identified forever. It was a sort of fingerprinting before fingerprinting; it was more like *body*printing. Bertillon calculated that if all the measurements were taken correctly, there was a 1 in 4,191,304 chance of one person being confused with another.

Bertillon was inspired by the tools of anthropometry—the study of the measurements of the human body. Anthropometry had a horrible history. It had been used to create a self-serving hierarchy of races, with Europeans at the top and everyone else at the bottom. It had been used to justify racist claims about groups. But Bertillon took a tool often used on other groups—other races, other cultures—and he applied it to the French themselves. He wasn't interested in groups or races. He was interested in *individuals*. He just wanted to be able to identify someone who'd escaped from prison.

His system was cumbersome and often vexing, but if the technicians were well trained, it was far better than no system at all. Now, thanks to Bertillon, the police could determine if a man claiming to be John Reynolds was actually Jack the Ripper.

The Bertillon system was only one of Bertillon's achievements. He standardized the mug shot and crime scene photography, achievements which alone would have secured his name in police history. Bertillon's fame was so great that he was described in a Sherlock Holmes story as the greatest detective in Europe. Sherlock Holmes himself was the *second* greatest.

Indeed, when the Bertillon system worked best, it felt straight out of fiction.

A dizzying example:

A decade or so before the *Mona Lisa* theft, a wealthy, respectable Parisian named Charles Vernet came under suspicion. The detective on his case, Marie-François Goron, a man with a truly fabulous mustache, was convinced that Vernet was an alias. He thought Vernet was actually a criminal named Simon, who'd killed someone a decade before.

Goron's theory had a couple of problems. First, Simon had been convicted of the murder and sentenced to twenty years of labor on Devil's Island, a French prison off the coast of South America. Also—and this was a sizable second problem—Simon was dead. Along with a partner, he'd escaped from Devil's Island, but he'd failed to make it to South America. A body had been found: it was unidentifiable, but it was wearing Simon's prison jacket and number.

But Goron wondered: What if Simon had killed his partner and switched jackets with him? What if Simon had staged his own death?

Goron believed that if he measured Vernet—if he used the Bertillon system—he could prove that Vernet was actually Simon. The police had Simon's measurements already. The measurements just had to match.

Vernet, however, was rich and well connected. Goron couldn't simply arrest him and measure him on the basis of an outlandish theory. He'd already been warned off investigating him. Instead, he'd have to trick Vernet.

An opportunity arrived in the form of a society party that Vernet planned to attend. The party would feature presentations on the latest scientific developments, including a newfangled invention called the cinematograph. Goron got himself invited to speak about the Bertillon system. When he stood up to talk, he explained that he'd be demonstrating this new science of identification. Could he have some volunteers?

As he measured a line of society elites, he saw Vernet slipping out of the room.

Goron had met Vernet before and now called out to him, "Monsieur Vernet, don't go away. Have your measurements taken."

Vernet could not simply run. Running would look bad;

running would look like an admission of guilt. He forced a smile and politely declined. "I've seen the thing done before," he said.

Goron subtly increased the pressure. "Ladies," he said to a pair of American girls standing near Vernet, "please take him into custody and bring him to me."

They laughed and seized Vernet, who was now the center of attention. "Is this meant for a joke?" he scowled.

Goron pretended to be playing a game: "It's part of the fun!"

Vernet gave in. Goron carefully measured him, the whole time pretending he was simply demonstrating the system. Then he quietly led Vernet to a separate room and arrested him. The measurements had matched: Vernet *was* Simon.

Vernet confessed soon afterward.

It was just what the evening had promised—a very public demonstration of the latest scientific developments. It was the sort of story that made the Bertillon system—and Bertillon himself—a legend.

THE NEW AGE OF SCIENTIFIC POLICING WAS BUILT ON NUMBERS. THAT'S WHAT convicted Vernet.

But there were no measurements for the thief of the *Mona Lisa*. And there was another sort of story about Alphonse Bertillon—a story that suggested that without good data, things would turn out far less happily.

This other story was the story of a humiliating failure. Louis Lépine needed to find the *Mona Lisa* because he was Louis

Lépine. But Alphonse Bertillon needed to find the painting to *become* Alphonse Bertillon again.

He'd fallen a long way.

About fifteen years before the *Mona Lisa* was stolen, the French government discovered a spy in its midst. Even worse, the spy was working for the German government, feeding the Germans information about the French military. It was treachery of the highest order.

Suspicion quickly focused on Captain Alfred Dreyfus, for a pair of extremely bad reasons. First, Dreyfus's handwriting looked very vaguely like the writing on a note that had been sent to the Germans. Second, Dreyfus was Jewish.

The second reason alone was enough. There was a wave of antisemitism in France, and antisemitic newspapers whipped readers into a hysteria. Mobs marched. Only the criminal conviction of Dreyfus could save France, it was said.

The French government was so desperate for a conviction that it forged evidence against Dreyfus. Its logic was: Dreyfus was guilty. Everyone knew that. The forged evidence would just make sure he was *found* guilty.

Alphonse Bertillon, who knew nothing about the forgery, testified at Dreyfus's trial. His job was to prove that Dreyfus's handwriting matched the incriminating note, and he took the stand with a bewildering display of charts and pseudoscientific diagrams. Bertillon was not a handwriting expert, but he was unshakably confident.

A fair trial was impossible. Dreyfus was convicted. The crisis was over.

Except that a couple of years later, the French government

discovered that the Germans were *still* getting inside information. It certainly wasn't coming from Dreyfus, who was then serving a life sentence on Devil's Island, Simon's former home.

The discovery threw France into chaos. Half the country believed that Dreyfus had been framed; the other half thought that Dreyfus should be put to death. Another trial was held, and Bertillon testified again, with the same absolute conviction. "The proof is there, and it is irrefutable," he told the court.

In fact, the proof was not there, and it was easily refutable. People in the courtroom laughed at Bertillon. Outsiders examined his evidence. Their verdict was not kind. Bertillon's evidence, they said, was evidence of nothing at all.

Dreyfus, unbelievably, was found guilty again. But it was now obvious that he was a victim, not a criminal. He'd soon be pardoned.

Bertillon emerged from the whole affair with a gravely damaged reputation. He'd assumed that Dreyfus was guilty. He'd expected that Dreyfus was guilty. He'd refused to change his mind.

Bertillon's work represented the beginning of forensic science. But the Dreyfus affair revealed a real danger hidden by the word *science*. Calling this sort of policing *science* could cover up what was actually going on, and what was actually going on was often just a mess of assumptions.

Assumptions dressed up as science.

Even the best investigators might not realize they were relying on assumptions. They might think they had actual clues.

They might go way, way down the wrong path.

IT TAKES A THIEF TO
CATCH A THIEF

THE DAY THE *MONA LISA* WAS DISCOVERED MISSING, THE *PARIS-JOURNAL* asked:

IS ARSÈNE LUPIN ALIVE?

MONA LISA *GONE FROM THE LOUVRE!*

Arsène Lupin was an infamous gentleman burglar with perfect cheekbones and manners. He preferred a tuxedo and a high black silk hat, but he was a master of disguise and an escape artist, and for years, he'd danced in circles around the authorities. The calling card of his crimes was their sheer, infuriating cleverness.

Lupin had a line he wouldn't cross: murder. Fantômas, on the other hand, would cross every line. He was a ruthless criminal—a holy terror, not a gentleman—and his name alone paralyzed the police. A single, murderous, bone-chilling word: Fantômas.

It was a terrifying time—or it would have been if Lupin and Fantômas had been real.

They weren't. They were characters in stories; they only existed on paper. But to many Parisians, Lupin and Fantômas seemed as alive as anyone on the street. Each new installment in their adventures sold as fast as it was printed. The public couldn't get enough.

In England, readers wanted detectives like Sherlock Holmes.

In France, readers took the side of thieves.

Lupin and Fantômas were so seemingly real that the line between fact and fiction became blurred. Maybe the *Mona Lisa* thief had been inspired by Arsène Lupin! Or maybe the thief *was* Arsène Lupin!

This confusion between what was real and what was imaginary shadowed the *Mona Lisa* investigation. But such mix-ups had started over a century before, with a different master of disguise.

His story was true. It was too strange to be anything but true.

BORN IN 1775—FIFTEEN YEARS BEFORE A REVOLUTION WOULD TEAR FRANCE apart—Eugène François Vidocq had a brief, disastrous career as a soldier.

He quit. He was better at crime.

The man had talent. He changed identities as easily as other people changed clothes, and if caught, he was almost impossible to keep in jail. He once escaped from a prison where the inmates wore heavy irons on their legs and arms at all times. But his luck ran out, and when he was caught a final time, Vidocq offered the police a deal: Release him, and he'd quit crime and go to work for *them*. He'd become an informant. He had contacts everywhere.

It was the best deal the authorities ever made.

Vidocq's scheme worked so well he convinced the Paris police to make him the head of a new undercover unit. For the first time, the police wouldn't look like police. They'd look like . . . well, no one would have any idea what they'd look like: eye-patched pirates, limping pickpockets, scarred swordsmen.

It was hugely successful, but the idea of having police who weren't dressed as police felt wrong to many officers. It felt especially wrong that this new branch of the law was staffed by people who'd broken the law. Vidocq didn't sometimes hire criminals. He *only* hired criminals. The saying "It takes a thief to catch a thief" wasn't just a saying for Vidocq—it was his whole strategy. "I preferred men whose record had given them a little celebrity," he once stated.

Many people were suspicious. If these men *used* to be criminals, maybe they still were. Maybe Vidocq was too! Maybe they were all breaking the law while simultaneously *being* the law!

Eventually, the suspicion was suffocating. Vidocq was pushed out. He got his revenge by founding the first private detective agency in the world. He was the first person to use any sort of scientific methods in policing. He matched bullets to guns; he used plaster casts to identify footprints. The forensic science that Bertillon and Lépine relied on was invented by Vidocq.

His story was irresistible. It inspired the American writer Edgar Allan Poe, who inspired Arthur Conan Doyle, who created Sherlock Holmes. In his epic novel *Les Misérables,* Victor Hugo used Vidocq as a model for both Jean Valjean *and* Inspector Javert—the convict *and* the law.

Vidocq led a life that sounded like fiction but was fact. And then the greatest writers of the age turned that fact into fiction. The line between fact and fiction was so blurry it was hard to see at all.

⌒

ALL THIS MEANT THAT WHEN LOUIS LÉPINE AND ALPHONSE BERTILLON INVEStigated the *Mona Lisa* theft, they did so alongside a police force of fictional detectives and a gang of fictional thieves.

Those fictional thieves—Lupin and Fantômas first among them—set a high standard. They were crafty and cunning; they were always several steps ahead of the law. Actual detectives like Lépine and Bertillon began to expect this sort of ingenuity from actual thieves, especially in the so-called superior, refined class of crimes.

Such thieves were noble adversaries. Any fool could solve a simple crime, the thinking went, but it would take a brilliant crime for a brilliant detective to truly show his worth.

A vivid example: the strangest jewel heists in history, the year before the *Mona Lisa* disappeared.

The crime itself was ordinary: precious jewels had been stolen from wealthy homes in Lyon, France. But instead of in the dark of night, the burglaries occurred in the middle of the day. Even more perplexingly, only a single item of jewelry had been taken each time. Countless jewels were left behind.

In each case, the thief had snuck in through a window on a high floor. But how? And in broad daylight?

The detective assigned to the case was Edmond Locard, an early criminologist. Locard's motto was *Every contact leaves a trace.* Locard believed in a brand-new method of identification: fingerprinting. (He'd even burned his own finger pads to see if his fingerprints would change. They didn't.)

Investigating the burglaries, Locard found prints—but they didn't look like any prints he'd seen before.

A lesser detective would have thought they were lousy prints. A lesser detective would have moved on to a case that made more sense.

Instead, Edmond Locard asked all Lyon organ-grinders— street performers who played a sort of portable organ—to report to the police station. Also, he added, they should bring their monkeys. Organ-grinders often performed alongside a captive monkey, who did tricks and collected money.

Locard didn't fingerprint the organ-grinders. He finger-printed the *monkeys*. He found an exact match.

The monkey went to the zoo. The owner went to prison.

In 1911, this sort of counterintuitive brilliance was expected of both thief and detective.

Lépine and Bertillon knew what they had to live up to.

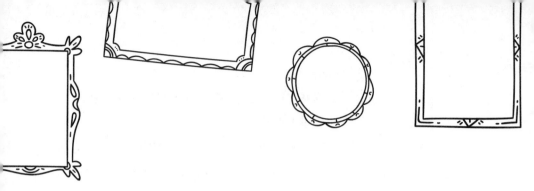

A BREAK IN THE CASE

THE THOUSANDS OF LEADS THE POLICE HAD RECEIVED ABOUT THE *MONA Lisa* were all false. They led nowhere.

But in the days after the theft, Alphonse Bertillon and Louis Lépine had managed to extract a couple of clues from the Louvre itself.

The first was the frame.

Remember the *Mona Lisa*'s antique frame, abandoned in the stairwell. Now ignore the frame. Focus on the glass—the controversial reflective pane.

A human being is covered with sweat glands: a square-inch section of the human hand contains thousands of them. These glands cool the body and lubricate the skin. When sweat passes through the skin, it leaves a precise record of whose body it passes through.

On the morning of Monday, August 21, everyone in Paris was

sweating. When the *Mona Lisa* thief put down the frame in the stairwell, he left the pattern of his sweat behind.

Like a magical mirror in a fairy tale, the glass would reflect the last person who held it. The glass would solve the crime it had witnessed.

The pane was hard and smooth, the perfect surface for a fingerprint, and Bertillon was extremely good at lifting prints. Once the frame was found, he knelt down beside it, holding it with a white handkerchief to protect it from his own fingerprints. With his other hand, he held a magnifying glass and slowly, methodically passed it over every last inch of the frame and glass.

The magnifying glass stopped halfway down the left side. There it was—a single moment in time and sweat, perfectly preserved.

Bertillon was only partly done. He took out a camel-hair brush, an exquisitely delicate tool, and brushed granite powder over the glass. Now he had a permanent record of the highly specific whorls and ridges. It was from a thumb, it turned out, and no other thumbprint would look just like it.

This technique—the use of fingerprinting to identify a person—was brand-new.

And Bertillon hated it.

Alphonse Bertillon believed he'd already solved the problem of identification with the Bertillon system, which had the advantage of being named after himself. His system worked well at identifying criminals with fake names and prior arrests, and it worked a lot better than the identification system it had replaced, which was no identification system at all.

But the Bertillon system had serious problems. It was incredibly difficult to implement: Different people measuring the same person sometimes got different measurements. It took time and skill to do well. Plus, there was the possibility that—though very rare—people could have the same Bertillon measurements.

Fingerprinting solved both problems.

The idea behind it—that every human has a unique fingerprint that cannot be altered—was proposed by the Scottish doctor Henry Faulds. For decades, Faulds tried and failed to convince someone, anyone, that he'd discovered a new system of identification. He was ignored for years, until finally his ideas were stolen from him (by Francis Galton, Charles Darwin's cousin). Then he was ignored again. For almost a century, the inventor of a way to identify people was never properly identified.

When Bertillon knelt down to lift a print off the frame of the *Mona Lisa,* his measurement method was being used across the world. But fingerprinting was on the rise, and it was beginning to displace the Bertillon system. Only a few years before, a

British murder case had been solved on the basis of nothing *but* fingerprints.

Bertillon had made detective work aspire to scientific standards. His own work was supposed to be detached and rigorous. But Bertillon was changing. He'd always been stubborn—that was clear from the Dreyfus affair—but now he was becoming a caricature of himself. He believed in *his* system, not these new-fangled fingerprints. Nevertheless, he agreed to add fingerprints to his Bertillon cards.

The problem was, the cards were still organized according to the measurements of the Bertillon system. In England, it was already possible to search by fingerprint; a complex system of classification meant that a new fingerprint could be compared to similar fingerprints on file in minutes. In Paris, because of Bertillon, fingerprints were unsearchable. The only way to match a fingerprint was to get lucky—and since there were almost a million entries in Bertillon's files, a detective would have to get *really* lucky.

But the fingerprint on the glass pane could still be useful. If Bertillon suspected someone, he could take their fingerprints and see if they matched.

He couldn't fingerprint all of Paris, though. He'd have to narrow it down.

Which was why the other clue was so important.

In the week after the theft, while the Louvre was closed, Bertillon arranged for another painting to be put in the *Mona Lisa's* place. This painting would be attached to the wall in the exact same way. Same frame. Same glass. Same hooks.

Then it would be stolen.

Bertillon staged a fake heist, a re-creation of the original theft.

His first set of "thieves" knew nothing about the Louvre, and they struggled to get the painting off the wall. They succeeded after an agonizing amount of time: five minutes. The Louvre was poorly guarded, and it was especially poorly guarded on a Monday morning at the height of August, but five minutes was a long time to spend prying a painting off a wall in any museum.

The second set of "thieves" worked at the Louvre and knew how the painting was hung on the wall. They were able to get it free in five seconds.

Five seconds.

The conclusion was obvious: it was an inside job.

EVERYTHING THAT IT IS POSSIBLE TO DO

IN WHICH LEONARDO SKIPS TOWN
AND FAILS TO SCULPT AN ENORMOUS HORSE

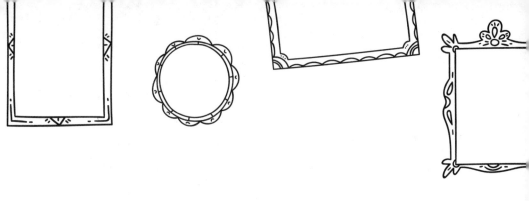

FLORENCE, 1481

FIFTEEN YEARS AFTER HE ARRIVES IN FLORENCE, LEONARDO RECEIVES A commission for another altarpiece, this time for a monastery just outside town. He's already famous for walking away from his work, so the contract requires Leonardo to finish the painting or get nothing.

Leonardo runs out of money before he even begins the altarpiece. He buys food and wine on credit. He borrows money just to buy paint. He decorates the monastery's clock in exchange for firewood.

Leonardo da Vinci is working for *sticks*.

Somehow, he delivers an extraordinary painting, the *Adoration of the Magi*. It's an old biblical scene, but Leonardo breathes new life into it. His version swells with emotion. It's enormous, almost eight feet by eight feet, and every inch is alive with movement.

Except—it isn't really a painting at all. It's a draft, what's called an *underpainting*.

Today this painting—this *under*painting—is among the most famous artworks in the Uffizi, the Florence museum stuffed with famous paintings. It has been called the most influential unfinished painting in all of art history.

It's unfinished because Leonardo abandons it. He's sick of Florence. He's a genius—everyone knows he's a genius—but he's also a failure. He can't get commissions, and when he does, he can't finish them. He cannot make himself stay in town, even to finish the altarpiece. Maybe *especially* to finish the altarpiece. He's already thought out the altarpiece, after all. For Leonardo, the patron saint of distraction, there's no need to finish it.

He packs up his rose robes. The Medicis, the ruling family of Florence, could convince him to stay; they could give him money and commissions. They do not.

Leonardo da Vinci, the great genius of the Florentine Renaissance, walks out of town.

He has his eye on Milan, the northern city-state run by Duke Ludovico Sforza. The duke is impatient and ambitious, and he spends money lavishly. He's collecting a court around him, a Milanese Renaissance.

Leonardo writes the duke a letter, asking to serve the court. The letter is a request for patronage, a sort of job application. In it, Leonardo lays out his résumé.

He makes it all up.

Knowing that the duke will welcome military expertise, Leonardo says that he's an engineer who can dig underground tunnels. (He isn't.) He says he can destroy any fortress, even a fortress founded on solid rock. (He can't.) He says he can construct cannons, catapults, and other machines of war. (He hasn't.) He says he can do the same for wars at sea. (He hasn't done that either.) He says he can make "armored vehicles" to attack enemy armies. (Did he say *armored vehicles?*)

"In short," Leonardo concludes modestly, "I can contrive an infinite variety of machines for attack or defense."

An *infinite variety.*

Now, Leonardo is Leonardo. It isn't wise to bet against him. Leonardo certainly has *plans* for many of these things. But he hasn't actually done any. The polite thing to say about this letter is that it is confident. The accurate thing to say is that it is delusional.

At the very end of the letter, Leonardo remembers something he can do: "Also I can undertake sculpture in marble, bronze, or clay, and in painting I can do everything that it is possible to do, as well as any other man whoever he may be."

Everything that it is possible to do.

That part of the letter is true.

⌐⟋

WHEN LEONARDO DA VINCI ARRIVES AT THE COURT OF MILAN, HE ISN'T INTRO-duced as a painter, or a sculptor, or an engineer, or even a mathematician.

He's introduced as a *musician.*

Leonardo is in fact a virtuoso of the lyre, a sort of early viola. He sings and improvises his own poems while he plays.

Today, there's a term for this range of talents: a *Renaissance man.* It means someone who's good at a whole lot of things that have nothing to do with each other. Leonardo is the original Renaissance man.

He knows how to make an impression. He appears before the Milan court with a silver lyre shaped like a horse's skull. He's made it himself. It is an extremely Leonardo thing to do.

It works. He receives a warm welcome in Milan.

MILAN IS NOT FAR FROM FLORENCE, LESS THAN TWO HUNDRED MILES TO THE north.

But in the fifteenth century, small distances are monumental. The language spoken in Milan sounds different; the landscape looks different. A visitor from Florence is a visitor from a faraway land. Milan is also bigger and busier than Florence. It's home to many scholars—mathematicians, philosophers, doctors. The exact people Leonardo wants to see.

Leonardo's music catches the fancy of the court. His letter draws the attention of the duke. He will stay in Milan for almost twenty years. He will paint there, but he will spend more time doing . . . well, everything else.

In Milan, Leonardo's notebooks begin to overflow.

Describe the jaw of crocodile.
Describe the beginning of a human when it is in the womb.
Describe how the clouds are formed, and how the they
    dissolve, and what causes vapor to rise from the waters
    of the earth into the air, and the causes of mists,
    and . . .
Tell me.

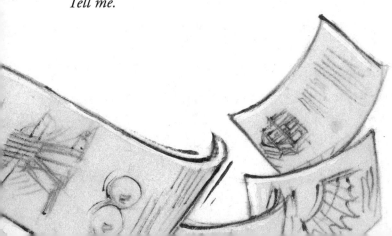

Leonardo doesn't think the way the people around him do. He starts with the world: he observes what's around him. Then he reasons: he finds a theory that explains his observations. Finally, he tests his theory.

Most people at the time work in the *opposite* direction. They don't start with the world; they start with the theory. For many people in the Renaissance, what makes something true is whether it makes sense *abstractly*. They believe you get to know the world by separating yourself from the world. They don't start with the world itself. They start with the world in their head.

But there's a problem with this method: The world in their head might be very different from the *actual* world. Their theory might end up being true in their head—but nowhere else.

Leonardo doesn't make this mistake. He always starts with the world: first, observe.

In Milan, he makes a meticulous record of the human body. Imagine him whirling around in his rose robes, a measuring string slung over his neck, calling out numbers. Every person is different, but Leonardo finds that their *proportions* are the same: "The space between the mouth and the base of the nose is one-seventh of the face. . . . The space from the mouth to the bottom of the chin is one-fourth of the face and equal to the width of the mouth." He goes on: "The great toe is the sixth part of the foot. . . . When the arm is bent, the fleshy part shrinks to two-thirds of its length. . . ."

By starting with specifics, he's discovered something far more general.

Was all this measurement, these minute observations, to help him paint better? No one else at the time thinks it is necessary. Michelangelo doesn't spend his time measuring people.

Maybe Leonardo is simply curious. He's entranced by physics and mathematics, by surgery and medicine, by philosophy and engineering. He sketches out endless ideas for inventions—a submarine here, a steam-powered cannon there. Few of these will ever exist. They are glimpses of what could be.

He thinks seriously about the problem of flight and jots down ideas for a helicopter. He designs a parachute. He may have tried to fly himself. A young mathematician in Milan writes that Leonardo did and *failed*. Regardless of whether he did or not, the temptation must have been enormous. There were new realms of knowledge in the air.

Down on the ground, he devises spectacles for the duke. This is a time of festivals and carnivals, of extraordinary theatrical pageants. Each extravaganza is expected to surpass its predecessors; no expense is spared.

Leonardo, as far as we can tell, enjoys this part of the job. He likes creating these special effects: the stranger and the harder, the better. In a notebook, he writes: "Boil ten pounds of brandy to evaporate, but see that the room is completely closed and throw up some powdered varnish among the fumes. Then enter the room suddenly with a lighted torch, and at once it will set ablaze."

He isn't angry that he isn't painting. He's Leonardo: he spends most of his time not painting anyway. He never lives for posterity, and he has no idea that future generations will mourn not having more artwork from him. Getting something done, making sure it will endure: people will say that these are not Leonardo's strengths. But that's unfair. It's more like these things aren't important to Leonardo.

He has enough on his mind, and in Milan, that mind is on fire. He's happy here. He's never leaving.

The odds of the *Mona Lisa* getting painted—the already long odds—grow slimmer still.

MILAN,
1493

N MILAN, LEONARDO IS COMMISSIONED TO SCULPT A STATUE OF A HORSE,
a tribute to the duke's father.

Leonardo sketches out a monumental statue, rising some twenty-five feet high. He decides to cast it in a single piece. It will require pouring eighty tons of melted metal in a single form. No one has done this before; it is not clear it can be done. Any flaw, any weakness, and the statue will crack. There is an easier way. Leonardo could cast the horse in pieces, and the pieces could be seamlessly joined. Since the horse is so large, it makes sense to cast it in pieces.

But Leonardo doesn't want to.

That's only part of the problem. The other part is that Leonardo wants his horse to be both larger than life and exactly *like* life. He wants every muscle, every vein, to be accurate. To do this, most artists would observe horses, and Leonardo does exactly that.

But he also dissects horses. Then he writes *an entire book* about horse anatomy.

This is all preparation.

Finally, Leonardo constructs a clay model of the horse, which he needs to make the mold for the casting, and the model becomes the wonder of Milan. So does Leonardo himself. "Neither Greece nor Rome ever saw anything grander," a Milan resident writes. "See how beautiful this horse is; Leonardo da Vinci alone has created it. Sculptor, fine painter, fine mathematician, so great an intellect rarely does Heaven bestow."

Everything is on schedule, which is to say everything is way behind schedule. It's Leonardo; there isn't really a schedule. But everything is good, everything is fine—until the French invade. Behind King Charles VIII, French armies pour down the Italian peninsula. After initially aiding Charles, the duke turns against him. To win the war, though, he needs more cannons. To make cannons, he needs more metal.

Imagine the duke looking around for bronze, the material he desperately needs, and discovering that some *eighty tons of it* are reserved for a statue of a horse.

The bronze is melted down. The cannons are made. The statue is not.

Leonardo is brokenhearted. In his papers, there's a letter he writes and does not send to the duke. It's torn in half. At the end, it reads:

And of the horse I will say nothing because I know the times . . .

Years later, when the French reach Milan, they use the clay model for target practice. It falls into a thousand pieces. It's a tragedy—but it is also a half decade since Leonardo got the commission.

When Michelangelo mocks Leonardo for not delivering the goods, this is what he seizes on: *You had eighty tons of bronze, and you still couldn't get that statue done, you fool.*

Michelangelo is being unfair. (Michelangelo is being a jerk. Everyone agrees that Michelangelo was a jerk.) The statue really was an unprecedented project.

But Michelangelo also has a point.

Leonardo had the time. He had the materials. He ended up with nothing.

FOR HIS NEXT ACT, LEONARDO STARTS WORK ON A MURAL IN A MILAN monastery. It's a depiction of the last meal that Jesus shares with his disciples, and Leonardo uses the mural to tell a story about how the disciple Judas betrays Jesus. The word *story* here is key. The characters in the mural, like characters in a movie, react to each other. As the story of Judas's betrayal works its way down the table, the mural itself seems to move.

Painting the mural takes Leonardo forever, of course. There are stories about him standing in front of the painting for days without touching his brush. Or arriving, adding a couple of brushstrokes, and then leaving. The head of the monastery, the prior, pesters Leonardo to hurry up already. The duke summons him to ask what's taking so long. Leonardo explains that he's been unable to find the right model for Judas. It's hard to find a face so wicked, he says. But, he adds mischievously, maybe he could simply use that pestering prior as a model.

The duke doubles over with laughter. The prior relents.

Finally, Leonardo finishes. He finishes! He really, actually, no buts about it, *finishes.*

However.

Just as he decided to cast the horse in a wholly new way, Leonardo decides to paint his mural in a wholly new way. The standard way to paint a fresco—a painting on a wall—is to use water-based paints on fresh plaster. Leonardo does not want to do this. In his paintings, he prefers oils, which allow him to work slowly. Fresh plaster does not allow for this leisure: he has to paint while the plaster is still wet.

Leonardo makes up his own technique as he goes along. He coats the dry plaster wall with primer and then uses a mixture of oil and water paints. It works: the fresco is incredibly subtle and layered. Leonardo has transferred his oil technique to fresco painting. No one has ever done it before.

No one will ever do it again.

Within a few decades, the paint begins to flake away. Then it falls off altogether. Within a half century, it is hardly there. It's described as a "muddle of blots."

Today, the only work of art in the world as mobbed as the *Mona Lisa* is *The Last Supper*. It is a wonder. But we can see it only because it has been restored—extensively. *The Last Supper* we see today is a re-creation.

We have only a glimpse of what Leonardo actually painted.

THE LAST SUPPER WILL CRUMBLE. THE HORSE WAS NEVER CAST. LEONARDO has completed a few paintings in Milan, and he's done a lot of thinking, but little has been left for the future.

When King Charles VIII and his French army finally reach Milan, the duke's court flees. Leonardo stays for six weeks, trying to see what the new possibilities are. He's playing both sides. It's a dangerous game, and Leonardo has not quite adjusted to it. In his notebooks, there's a strange sentence: "Find Ingil and tell him that you will wait for him at Amor and that you will go to him at Ilopan."

Ingil, Amor, Ilopan: these are all names written backward. *Ingil* is Ligni, or the Count de Ligny, the French military chief. *Amor* is Roma, or Rome. *Ilopan* is Napoli, or Naples.

This is Leonardo—among the most brilliant minds of his era—writing in code. His code is simply to write the words backward. It must be the worst code in the history of codes. A dolphin could decipher this code.

It gets even worse. Leonardo's handwriting is a mirror script—he writes everything in the opposite direction and backward. (It's called *mirror script* because if you put Leonardo's writing in front a mirror, it's reversed and perfectly readable.) Mirror script is often thought to be a code of its own. It's not. At the time, it was a known way for left-handers to write

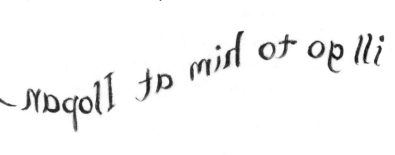

more comfortably. (That way, they wouldn't smear the ink as they moved their writing hand across the page.) But for this coded note, it has an unintended side effect: since Leonardo was already writing backward, all these backward names are written *forward*.

Amor isn't in mirror script. It's just Roma. Anyone can read it. You don't even have to hold it in front of a mirror.

All of this is very charming and very human. Leonardo da Vinci: he does boneheaded things just like the rest of us.

His flirtation with the French does not last. Leonardo flees Milan too. "Sell what you cannot take with you," he writes. He takes his half-finished work of almost twenty years, piles it into a cart, and leaves for Florence.

Leonardo has to abandon the city where he came into his own. He has to flee back to a city that he'd already fled from. He's almost fifty years old. He's homeless.

⌒☉

THE INVADING KING CHARLES VIII OF FRANCE WAS FOOLISH AND RECKLESS. He's mostly known today for marrying a woman who was already married and for dying from hitting his head on a doorframe.

But we owe him.

Without him, Leonardo would likely have never left Milan. Without him, the *Mona Lisa* would have never existed.

THE CONSUMMATE PROFESSIONAL

IN WHICH THE LOUVRE REOPENS TO MASSIVE CROWDS AND THE POLICE GO IN SEARCH OF A DEAD MAN

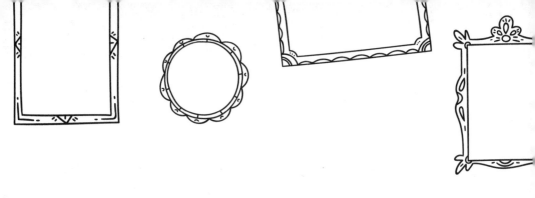

THE LOUVRE REOPENS

FOR OVER A HUNDRED YEARS, THE LOUVRE HAD BEEN A QUIET PLACE.
Before 1911, only a few hundred people visited each day, and fewer in summer. They vanished into a complex the size of a small city. The Louvre could be open and feel like it was closed.

That was about to change.

After a week of police occupation, the Louvre reopened to the public.

Paris had been spellbound by breathless *Mona Lisa* coverage. Now Parisians swarmed the scene of the crime. They came by the thousands. There had never been lines at the Louvre before. Suddenly, the lines went around the block. The Louvre had never seen such crowds.

They were all there to see something that *couldn't* be seen. The visitors who filed into the Salon Carré didn't look at the extraordinary paintings still in the room. They looked at where another painting *used* to be. People came to the Louvre to see a ghost. A journalist did a survey: most people there had never seen the *Mona Lisa* before. In other words, they'd come to not see a painting that they'd never seen.

Bouquets were laid. Notes were left. Tears were shed. The Louvre felt less like a museum and more like a funeral home.

The scene repeated itself daily for weeks. The missing *Mona Lisa* became a tourist attraction. It even attracted the young, depressive Franz Kafka, soon to be a great writer, now aimlessly wandering around Europe. He and his friend Max Brod did the full *Mona Lisa* tour: they stared at the blank wall and then they went to a silent comic film on the theft. The *Mona Lisa* was already a movie star.

In the short film, the Louvre administration is incompetent, the police are inept, and the museum is in pandemonium. There's so much chaos that no one notices when the thief brings the *Mona Lisa* back. He leaves a note: "Blame my poor eyesight. I wanted the painting next to her."

Franz Kafka liked the movie.

The incompetence of the Louvre was now a national joke. In the newspaper *L'Intransigeant,* the modernist poet Guillaume Apollinaire praised the portrait: "The Mona Lisa was so beautiful that her perfection has come to be taken for granted." Then he attacked the museum. "There is not even one guard per gallery. The situation is one of carelessness, negligence, indifference." The Louvre, he concluded, with an insult designed to puncture French pride, "is less well protected than a Spanish museum."

When the museum reopened, the *Paris-Journal* printed a sign to post in the galleries:

In the Interest of Art
And for the Safeguarding of the Precious Objects
THE PUBLIC
Is Requested to be Good Enough to
WAKE THE GUARDS
If They Are Found to be Asleep

Outside the Louvre, the *Mona Lisa* appeared in advertisements for underwear. Her face was on chocolate boxes and posters for variety shows. She hawked cigarettes. She performed in cabarets. Songs were rewritten in her honor.

A week after the theft, the *Mona Lisa* herself wrote to the *L'Autorité* newspaper. She was bored, she announced, with all this talk about her smile. She was not smiling mysteriously. She was smiling because she was filled with contempt—for all the people who "paraded endlessly in front of me." She had long desired, she wrote, to "carry out my abduction."

According to the *Mona Lisa,* the *Mona Lisa* had kidnapped herself.

The story of the theft spread far beyond Paris. It went global. From the United States: "The entire world sat back aghast. Nothing like the theft of the Mona Lisa had ever been perpetrated before in the world's history." From Canada: "The eyes of the world have been, in the past two weeks, trying to follow the sensational flight, by theft, of the Mona Lisa." From Australia: "Energetic searchings continue for Leonardo da Vinci's 'La Joconde.'" From England, with typical understatement: "There appears to be much mystery associated with the affair."

The timing was just right. Newspapers could now print illustrations cheaply and well, and they all ran illustrated supplements on the theft. The *Mona Lisa* became the most prominent face in the world, staring out of every newsstand. (In France after the theft, more people could identify the *Mona Lisa* than the president of the country.) These reproductions were like the new, unnerving world of cinema—an image of something that no longer existed.

The world could now see the *Mona Lisa* everywhere *but* the Louvre.

THE INGENIOUS THIEF

ALPHONSE BERTILLON HAD A PRINT—A PERFECT THUMBPRINT—BUT nothing else.

The Louvre employed almost three hundred people, and many more had worked there or might know how its paintings were hung. The Paris police had to cast a wide net. They were interviewing every last person, but it was easy to see how someone might wiggle free. So far, there were no solid leads, and even worse, there were no matching prints.

Without clues, the investigation didn't know who or what to focus on. In the absence of anything real, the same sort of stock characters kept coming up. These were *types* of people, like generic actors in a bad movie, but these imaginary people drove the investigation: they affected how the police thought about who was guilty, who was innocent, and who was worth another look.

The first character: the Secret Admirer.

The Secret Admirer was the *Mona Lisa* lover so bewitched that he (it was always a *he*) stole the painting out of obsession. The German young man arrested early in the investigation— the Louvre visitor who'd been a little too interested in the *Mona Lisa*—was a classic Secret Admirer type. That alone was enough to make him suspicious. The idea of the infatuated Secret Admirer loomed large throughout the investigation.

The second: the Lone Madman.

The authorities worried that the thief was *insane* or *crazy*— this was the language they used. Their logic was simple: only someone insane would try to steal the *Mona Lisa*, so the *Mona Lisa* must have been stolen by someone who was, well, insane. It was a theory composed entirely of circular logic, but it was at least a theory.

Finally, there was the third, and the most promising character: the Consummate Professional.

The Consummate Professional was able to steal the *Mona Lisa* because he was the Consummate Professional: experienced, meticulous, motivated. The scale of the theft was a job for a Consummate Professional, not a Secret Admirer or a Lone Madman. Or maybe the Consummate *Professionals:* The theft was too big to be the work of a single person. Instead, it might be a gang—a gang of professional art thieves.

In 1911, stealing art was still new. Until recently, art hadn't been stolen—it had been pillaged. When Napoleon, the French emperor, invaded Italy at the end of the eighteenth century, he arrived with lists of what he wanted: hundreds of paintings, prints, sculptures. His army stacked it up and shipped it out. It was a stupendous haul, and it wasn't a secret. It was all done out in the open. Then it was all put on display: Most of the Italian art in the Louvre had been stolen by Napoleon. The Salon Carré was lined with his plunder.

Art was stolen by *nations.* Random people stealing art: that was something different.

To Lépine and Bertillon, the idea of professional art thieves must have made the investigation more exciting. Such criminals would be worthy opponents. They would be people of the same high quality as Lépine and Bertillon themselves. From the beginning of the investigation, Lépine favored the idea.

We can guess what Lépine was thinking. Earlier that year, he'd written the introduction to a book on the new scientific policing. The book was by one of his former assistants, and it provides a window into how Bertillon and Lépine thought.

Just like society, crime was separated into classes, the book explained. There were classes of thieves: those who specialized in "audacious, difficult, profitable" thefts, and those whose work was "brutal and bloody." The superior thieves worked with "a refinement of art." The lower-class thieves, on the other hand, were sloppy; they left clues and devastation in their wake. The police, upon arriving at a crime scene, could tell immediately which class was responsible.

If the scene was gory, messy, or clumsy, it was the work of the lower class. If the scene was elegant, sophisticated, or crafty, it was the work of the upper class. Plug in your adjectives and get your thief. It was as easy as that.

Except, of course, it wasn't. This wasn't good detective work.

In fact, it wasn't detective work at all—there was no *detection* involved. It was all *assumption.* It was the opposite of observation, the opposite of how Leonardo would have wanted the *Mona Lisa* theft investigated. Unlike Leonardo, Bertillon and Lépine didn't start with the world. They started with what they *assumed* the world to be. They confused that with the *actual* world.

Lépine was looking for a professional gang because it would represent a superior class of thief. His logic was: The *Mona Lisa* heist was a refined crime. There was no blood on the walls of the Louvre. Therefore, it was done by a better class of criminal.

This type of thinking was so convincing that it led the investigation to some very strange places.

It led to the graveyard.

⌒♫

LONG BEFORE THE *MONA LISA* BROKE OUT OF THE LOUVRE AND MADE HER WAY onto the front page, Adam Worth was a celebrity.

To call him a thief sold him short. To police in the United States and Europe, he was *the* thief. For decades before the *Mona Lisa* theft, he'd been suspected of every con, every forgery, every eccentric scheme: if the job was brilliant, it might be the work of Adam Worth.

In the Sherlock Holmes stories, Alphonse Bertillon was the greatest detective in Europe. But Professor Moriarty—the archenemy of Holmes—was the greatest villain. "He is the organizer of half that is evil and of nearly all that is undetected in this great city," Holmes said. "He is a genius, a philosopher, an abstract thinker."

Professor Moriarty was based on Adam Worth.

Worth came from nothing. A poor immigrant to the United States, he deserted the Union army during the American Civil War, faked his own death, and began a relentless rise to the top of the criminal world. He lived by his wits, not his fists; he never tolerated violence. The mark of a Worth job was impeccable planning, and he applied the same rigor to his own life: he carefully acquired all the qualities of a gentleman and moved to England, where he held court in a London mansion.

He looked like a law-abiding upper-class Englishman to everyone but the authorities. They knew exactly who he was. But they never had enough evidence to arrest him. He never made a mistake.

"All that I ever require is two minutes of opportunity," Worth once said. "If I do not find those two minutes, I give up the job. Usually I find them, and 120 seconds, methodically employed, is enough for a man well-trained in his specialty to accomplish a great deal."

In 1876, after a series of brilliant bank heists and forgeries, he pulled off his greatest trick. He stole *Georgiana, Duchess of Devonshire,* by Thomas Gainsborough, the most famous painting in England.

The duchess was the great beauty of her age. She'd bewitched England while she was alive, and on canvas she had the same magnetic effect. The *Mona Lisa* of its day, the portrait was also famous for its smile, or *half* smile. Was it a smile? Was she looking at you? Was she flirting with you? You could hope. You could dream.

Duchess of Devonshire had just sold for more money than any painting ever, and it was about to be sold for even *more* money to the American millionaire Junius Spencer Morgan.

Before it could be sold, Worth stole it. In the middle of the night. Without a trace.

Then he did something curious: nothing at all. He didn't sell the painting. He didn't even try to sell it. He carried the *Duchess* around the world with him, often sleeping next to it.

The *Duchess* theft was the greatest art heist in history until the *Mona Lisa* went missing. The parallels were uncanny. A beautiful woman. A legendary portrait. A smitten thief. A crime that showed patience and daring. A crime that defied logic. A crime carried out by a superior class of thief.

Everything suggested that the *Mona Lisa* theft was the handiwork of Adam Worth, the gentleman thief.

A French novelist explained in *Le Figaro* that the painting could *only* have been stolen by Adam Worth. The theory caught fire. The US government told its officials on the Canadian border to watch for Worth smuggling the portrait into the United States. Everyone was on watch for Adam Worth.

There was only one problem: Adam Worth was dead.

Extremely dead. He'd died the decade before the *Mona Lisa* was stolen.

It was an inconvenient fact, because Adam Worth matched

the Paris police's idea of the thief perfectly. He *was* the Consummate Professional. He'd created the template for an epic art heist; he'd made the mold. What the police wanted was someone who fit that mold.

If Adam Worth wasn't available, they'd find someone else.

MARRY OR ELSE

IN WHICH BLOOD FLOWS THROUGH FLORENCE'S STREETS AND THE *MONA LISA* ALMOST SLIPS THROUGH HISTORY'S FINGERS

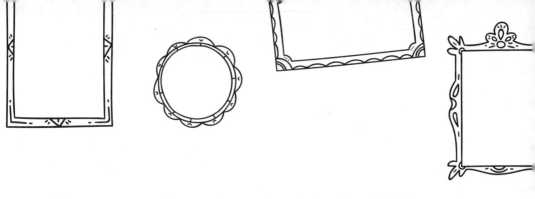

FLORENCE, 1494

I N FLORENCE, THE CLOCK IS TICKING.

Lisa Gherardini is fifteen. She's still living at home. She can't stay there for much longer. She has another five years. Maybe six at the most.

In Renaissance Florence, marriage comes early—as young as fifteen, but no later than twenty or so. It's the most important event in a Renaissance woman's life, and families spend years saving money for it. This money is called a dowry. Often, families make a down payment on a dowry at birth, so the money has years to accumulate interest before marriage. This is crucial, because in the late fifteenth century the cost of a dowry is rapidly inflating: the size of a respectable dowry is growing wildly each year. Even wealthy Florentines don't have enough money lying around.

Because Renaissance women don't work—the thought is unthinkable—the dowry helps support them in their new family.

Plus, a dowry, especially a generous dowry, is a sign of respectability.

There are strict rules:

No marrying without a dowry—that just isn't done.

No marrying someone who doesn't demand a dowry—that also isn't done.

No *not* marrying and staying at home—that would be humiliating to your family. An unmarried woman is a stain on a family's reputation. There are no single women in Florence. The city is like a horror movie: women who don't marry just *vanish*.

The rule is: *Marry or else.*

Else means a convent. That's where unmarried Florentine women go when they vanish. The nunneries around Florence are filled with girls without dowries. They spend their entire lives there, cut off from society. Beyond the old age of twenty lies the convent.

The path for Lisa Gherardini is straightforward. She will take her dowry and her beauty and settle down with a husband.

Except that Lisa Gherardini has no dowry.

Except that Lisa Gherardini is doomed.

This is not the life she is supposed to have, and to understand how it came to this, we have to look back to the time of Lisa's birth, a time of blood and revolution.

LISA GHERARDINI IS THE DAUGHTER OF LUCREZIA DEL CACCIA AND ANTONmaria di Noldo Gherardini, a Florentine nobleman with a distinguished family history. As a nobleman, Antonmaria did not work; he collected rent and goods from the peasants who tended his land in the countryside. It was a good household for Lisa to be born into.

It was not good enough.

On a spring morning in 1478, Lorenzo de' Medici, or Lorenzo the Magnificent, and his brother Giuliano, the golden boy of the Medici family, arrived for Mass at the Duomo, the iconic Florence cathedral.

The Medici brothers, who ruled Florence, were unimaginably prosperous and powerful. They were among the most formidable men in Europe, living proof of the rebirth of Florence. Standing in the Duomo, itself proof of Florentine genius, the brothers must have seemed untouchable.

In a few minutes, one would be dead.

At the height of the Mass, as they lowered their heads in prayer, Lorenzo and Giuliano were attacked from behind by their own companions. From the other direction—the altar—priests advanced on the Medici brothers. Cloaks and priestly robes parted to reveal swords and daggers. Giuliano fell in a frenzy of stabbing. Lorenzo, seriously wounded but not slain, escaped out a side door.

It was the beginning of a coup.

The Medicis had powerful enemies. The coup was the work of rival Florentine families, especially the Pazzis, as well as Pope Sixtus IV, a sworn Medici foe. Once the attack was underway, the Pazzis expected support from the Florentine people—they thought the assassinations would spark a revolution.

They were wrong. It was a fatal miscalculation.

The people of Florence did not rise up: given the choice of

the Pazzis or the Medicis, they chose the family they knew best (and feared most). Within hours, the coup had floundered, and instead of seizing power, the Pazzis were themselves seized. They were then hanged, their bodies dangling from the Florentine town hall for all to see. It was a grisly sight. It was a warning.

In the violent days that followed, hundreds more were killed. After the head of the Pazzi family was tortured and hanged, his dead body was dug up, thrown into a city ditch, dragged through the streets, hanged *again,* whipped, and then, finally, tossed, like a piece of rubbish, into the Arno River. So many deaths were inflicted, wrote the Italian philosopher Niccolò Machiavelli later, that "the streets were filled with limbs of men."

This was life in Renaissance Florence: scenes of unspeakable violence sitting side by side with the highest achievements of art and science. In an extraordinary combination of these extremes, a young Leonardo da Vinci stood at the base of the Florentine town hall and sketched a Pazzi conspirator hanging lifeless above him.

Pope Sixtus IV was outraged, but not by the violence—he'd sponsored the coup, after all. He was outraged that he hadn't won. In revenge, he cut Florence off from the Roman Catholic Church. Mass and Holy Communion—the core acts of worship in Catholicism—were now banned in Florence. Furthermore, the pope declared, the Medicis, and all of their supporters, were no longer Catholic at all. For good measure, he also claimed all Medici money and property in Rome.

But Pope Sixtus IV was not done. His papal forces joined with the Kingdom of Naples, and together their armies marched on Florence. They did not step lightly on the land. Everywhere they passed through, they turned to ashes. The destruction was total—including the rural property of a certain Florentine nobleman.

"For love of war," Antonmaria di Noldo Gherardini wrote that year, "I have no income. Our houses have been burned, our possessions smashed, and our workers and livestock lost."

He was left with nothing. Almost nothing: his wife was pregnant.

Lisa Gherardini was born the next year.

LORENZO DE' MEDICI MAKES PEACE WITH NAPLES. FLORENCE—OR AT LEAST the Medici family—is saved. But things improve very slowly for Antonmaria, and when Lisa is born, he has no money to set aside for a dowry. He deposits nothing. Lisa gets older. There is still nothing for her dowry.

Lisa is left with nothing but a future in a convent.

A place where only other nuns will see her face.

A place where she'll be all but invisible.

The *Mona Lisa* is slipping away.

GIGANTIC FIGURES IN HUMAN SHAPE

IN WHICH RICH AMERICANS SWARM EUROPE AND LEONARDO TELLS A JOKE

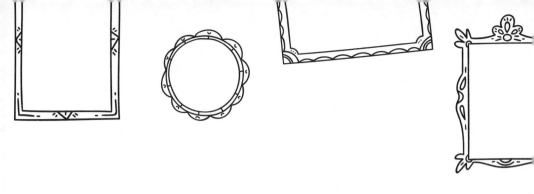

THE RICH AMERICAN

THE THEORY OF THE CONSUMMATE PROFESSIONAL HAD A FLAW.

Technically, it had a couple of flaws. The first was that Adam Worth was dead. (It was a significant flaw.)

The other was: Who buys the painting? The Consummate Professional steals the painting. But then who buys a painting that's so obviously stolen—so obviously *hot*?

The Consummate Professional would have anticipated this problem. He would have realized that the theft of the *Mona Lisa* would cause a stir.

Adam Worth himself had known this. When he targeted Gainsborough's *Duchess of Devonshire,* he had a specific goal: to blackmail its owner into paying the bond for his imprisoned brother. He never planned to sell the painting; he wanted it only to spring his brother from jail. (He kept it because his brother got out without his help.)

Worth never sold the *Duchess* because he knew it would be almost impossible to find the right buyer. He'd need to find someone who was both crooked and honest: Crooked enough to buy a stolen painting. Honest enough for to be trusted with the transaction.

It was a very hard needle to thread.

"It is generally conceded," Louis Lépine noted, "that even a dull person would realize the impossibility of selling such a famous work."

But there was a way to solve this problem, and Lépine knew it. What if the Consummate Professional already had a buyer lined up? What if the Consummate Professional had stolen the painting *for* someone? What if the whole thing was a contract job?

Introducing another stock character: the Rich American.

This was the end of the Gilded Age, a time when fortunes were amassed overnight, and the new twentieth century was awash in new money. A vastly unequal society had been born, with the rich and the poor farther apart than ever before. Nowhere was this more true than the United States, where the economy was dominated by a group of men so small in number that they could sit at the same table.

These men all wanted the same thing: they wanted their new money to look *old*.

Sure, they'd made their fortunes by paying starvation wages, and by busting union strikes, and by ruthlessly driving their competitors into the ground. But they didn't want it to look that way. They wanted their wealth to look respectable. So they founded philanthropies to give part of it away. And with the rest of it, they bought mansions and antiquities and art.

Lots and lots of art.

American millionaires came to Europe with their pockets full of cash and left with their arms full of paintings. They especially wanted paintings that would represent their own greatness. They wanted Great Paintings, by Great Artists. A Rich American commissioning a Consummate Professional to steal a Great Painting made perfect sense. The Rich Americans had made their money through all sorts of not-really-legal business. Why would they worry about a little not-really-legal business now?

The theory—a Rich American commissioning a Consummate Professional to steal a Great Painting—caught fire. "The belief is very general," the *New York Times* reported, "that the Florentine masterpiece is now in America."

And if it was in the United States, the theory went, it must be with J. P. Morgan.

The American businessman J. P. Morgan was indescribably rich and powerful—in fact, he made adjectives like *rich* and *powerful* look small. He'd held the US economy in his hand for the last half century. He'd done more than anyone else, including the US government itself, to shape that economy. With his fortune, Morgan lived in splendor at a massive scale: When his daughter was married, the reception was for a thousand people, and Morgan had it at his *house*. His homes doubled as museums.

When the *Mona Lisa* was stolen, Morgan was next door in Italy. Shortly afterward, he boarded a train in Florence with a painting among his trunks—and he was immediately mobbed by a crowd who assumed the painting was the *Mona Lisa*. Morgan had to fight his way onto the train with his cane.

The newspapers were flooded with rumors about Morgan. It

was reported that he'd met with "mysterious visitors" who'd sold him the *Mona Lisa*. The press hounded Morgan until he was forced to acknowledge the rumors.

"I have not been offered *Mona Lisa*," he told reporters, "and I regret it. Had it been offered, I should have bought it and given it back to France."

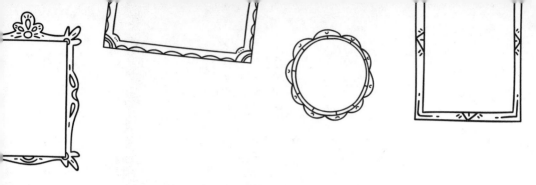

DR. NO
(PART 1)

F OR A MOMENT, LET'S LEAVE 1911 AND SNAP BACK TO THE PRESENT.
We're only here for the view. Because from here, we can
look down through the last century and see the fallout of a
single theory: the Rich American commissioning a Consummate Professional to steal a Great Painting.

Because of this theory, stealing art became different from
other sorts of stealing. It became a mark of sophistication. It
became *glamorous*.

Since a famous painting couldn't be sold, it could only be
appreciated. Who would want a painting that could only be appreciated? Only those able to appreciate. Only the most refined.

In the decades after the *Mona Lisa* theft, this theory would
get compressed. The Rich American and the Consummate Professional would merge into the same person: the Rich, Consummate Professional. The person who wanted the painting would
pull off the job himself. It was the ultimate superior class of
thief.

Today, the Rich, Consummate Professional appears in many movies. He steals paintings to enjoy in the privacy of his mansion. He's dashing and handsome, and he wears a well-tailored suit that fails to hide his muscles. He plays polo, or he knows how to play polo, or he knows people who play polo.

Everything about this story is wrong.

Art heists are almost always the work of amateurs, and there's nothing dashing or romantic about these thieves. They have no mansions or polo ponies. They're more likely to bungle the job than get it right.

⌐⟋

HERE'S A MORE ACCURATE, AND MORE ODD, STORY ABOUT WHO STEALS ART:

On August 21, 1961, in London—fifty years to the day after the *Mona Lisa* vanished—a portrait of the Duke of Wellington disappeared.

It had already been an exhausting few months for the duke. The portrait, painted by the great Francisco Goya some 150 years before, had been sold to an American millionaire. Newspapers in England howled at the sale. How could this very English portrait leave England? It was part of the country's cultural heritage. It couldn't be sold—and especially not to an American millionaire.

The duke stayed. The American millionaire was repaid. The painting went on display in the National Gallery in London. Less than a month later, it disappeared. There were no clues. It was a flawless job.

A week later, a ransom letter arrived. It began: "Query not that I have the Goya."

Query not!

The newspapers swooned. Such ornate language, people said, meant that the thieves must be men of intelligence and sophistication. Scotland Yard, the home of the London police, was flooded with tips. *The Duke of Wellington* became the *Mona Lisa* of 1961: everywhere but where he was supposed to be.

Like the *Mona Lisa,* the duke even became a movie star. In the very first James Bond film, released a year after the theft, Bond meets Dr. No in his evil lair. In the hideout, Bond walks past a painting on an easel. He does a double take. He's looking at Goya's *Duke of Wellington.*

The Rich, Consummate Professional was Dr. No himself.

Years pass. More ransom letters arrive. But the duke still doesn't show up.

In 1965, a man with bushy hair walks into a railway station in Birmingham, England. He hands the luggage clerk a package wrapped in brown paper. "Be very careful with this," he says. It is weeks before Scotland Yard realizes that *The Duke of Wellington* is lying on a rack in the Birmingham station luggage office.

The thief turns out to be a sixtysomething unemployed truck driver named Kempton Bunton. He didn't steal the Goya to enjoy it in his mansion. He stole the painting because he thought that the price for television licenses—the tax that funded British television and radio—was too high.

The tax in 1961 was fourteen dollars. Kempton Bunton had stolen a Goya over a fourteen-dollar fee. Kempton Bunton was not a man of intelligence and sophistication. Kempton Bunton was a bit bonkers.

Asked about his brilliant theft, Bunton said it was easy: he'd come in through the bathroom window. "The guards were having a cup of tea or were asleep," he explained.

Kempton Bunton was a deeply disappointing thief.

But here's the thing: Because he was so disappointing, the fact of Kempton Bunton disappeared without a trace. The idea of Dr. No remained. It's never gone away. Dr. No, the fictional character, seems more real to us than the very real Kempton Bunton.

It's a better story, after all. People will choose the better story every time.

In 1911, art theft was still new. Hollywood wasn't even an industry. But somehow the story of the brilliant art thief *already existed*. A half century before Dr. No appeared on screen, Louis Lépine and Alphonse Bertillon were already looking for him.

They weren't looking for a thief. They were looking for a story.

⌒‿⌒

LEONARDO WRITES ABOUT THIS EXACT SAME PHENOMENON—CONFUSING A *story* with a *person*.

Scattered throughout Leonardo's notebooks are riddles. Leonardo calls them *prophecies*, or glimpses of the future, and they're basically jokes with morals attached. They mock sloppy thinking. The moral is almost always: Look again. Look harder. Just because something *seems* doesn't mean that it *is*.

Here's a riddle that Leonardo writes down:

There will appear gigantic figures in human shape, but the nearer you get to them, the more their immense stature will diminish.

Hundreds of years later, the riddle reads like a clue. Not just any clue. The clue that Louis Lépine and Alphonse Bertillon were missing.

The *Mona Lisa* theft was gigantic. So Lépine and Bertillon were looking for a gigantic figure.

But what if the figure just *appeared* gigantic?

Leonardo's answer to his riddle was:

The shadow cast by a man at night with a lamp.

What if the thief was ordinary? What if he only looked large because of the *Mona Lisa*? What if the *Mona Lisa* was the lamp that made the thief appear gigantic?

WILL YOU BUY IT?

ACROSS THE ENGLISH CHANNEL, SHORTLY AFTER THE *MONA LISA* DISappeared from the Louvre, a man walked into the Duveen Brothers gallery in London.

From his office, Henry Duveen, an owner of the gallery, could hear the man arguing with an assistant. The man was demanding to see Henry Duveen himself.

Normally, no one raised their voice in the gallery. It was the premier art gallery in London, a sober, serious place. At least it was on the surface. Underneath, it was a ruthless, relentless business. Half the paintings leaving Europe for the United States seemed to pass through the gallery.

"Europe has a great deal of art," Henry's nephew Joseph Duveen once said, "and America has a great deal of money." It wasn't an observation; it was a business plan. Europe was full of minor nobles with more culture than money. The Duveens bought their best paintings and sold them to people with more money than culture: Rich Americans.

The Duveens were extremely good at it. The idea that the rich would want to spend money on old, odd works of art—that was an idea the Duveens helped establish.

They were very clever. Unlike Louis Béroud, the Duveens *wanted* their clients to see their own reflections. Literally. Before showing a painting, the Duveens would apply a heavy coat of varnish to it. Their clients were vain; they were delighted to see themselves in a masterpiece. The varnish shone. The clientele glowed. The painting sold.

Like the Louvre itself, the Duveen Brothers gallery in London was a place that every Rich American passed through. Those Americans, however, did not raise their voices.

Henry Duveen went out to see what the fuss was.

"I must see you alone and at once," said the man. He wasn't polished or moneyed; he wasn't the usual Duveen client. "It is a very important matter."

Duveen took the man to his office, mostly so he'd stop making a scene. Once the office door closed, the man asked: "Will you give me your word of honor that you will never reveal what I am going to tell you?"

"Of course," Duveen said impatiently. "Of course."

"Now listen," the man went on, "I have the *Mona Lisa* here in London. Will you buy it?"

Henry Duveen's mouth fell open.

"Well, what do you say?" the man insisted. "What's the figure you'll give me?"

It was a fraud, Duveen assumed. It *had* to be a fraud. But he also feared it might be something far worse: the truth.

Henry Duveen needed to stay far away from the *Mona Lisa*

theft. Who knew what rumors might get started about his involvement? If his reputation were stained, the gallery would be ruined. If this man truly had the *Mona Lisa,* he was a threat to Duveen's whole existence.

Duveen's mind spun. He stared at the man. Duveen spent his days talking people into buying art, but here, faced himself with the possibility of buying the most valuable work of art on the market, he was speechless. If he said yes, then he'd be part of a criminal conspiracy; if he said no, then he'd have to report the conversation to the authorities—he'd be a witness in the investigation, and Henry Duveen wanted to be nowhere near this investigation.

Then, finally, he saw a third option: He said neither yes nor no; he *laughed.* He laughed loudly, as if the whole conversation were a joke: *The* Mona Lisa*! What nonsense! What next?* He turned his back and walked away.

The man on the other side of his desk had once disappeared into Paris.

Now he exited the Duveen Brothers gallery and disappeared into London.

The *Mona Lisa* was gone.

AN IMPROBABLE SERIES OF IMPROBABLE EVENTS

IN WHICH LEONARDO GETS A JOB AND LISA GHERARDINI, AGAINST ALL ODDS, BECOMES THE *MONA LISA*

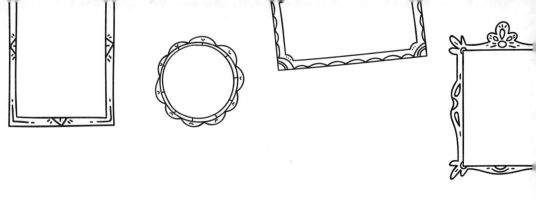

FLORENCE, 1495

FRANCESCO DEL GIOCONDO NEEDS A WIFE, AND SOON.

A successful Florentine silk merchant and trader, Francesco was recently widowed and has a young son. He has money. He has promise. He can choose any number of girls flush with cash from prominent families.

Marriage in Renaissance Florence is not about love. It's a practical affair. A marriage with a bad dowry is automatically a bad marriage.

Lisa Gherardini has a very bad dowry. She has no dowry at all.

But Francesco and Antonmaria, Lisa's father, know each other. Instead of a dowry, Antonmaria offers Francesco some property, the deed to a farm outside Florence. Francesco will receive the whole estate, with all its land and livestock. It's a highly unusual dowry.

But Francesco takes the offer.

We have no idea why.

Lisa has no choice in the marriage. (That's normal for the time.) When they wed, Francesco is thirty years old and Lisa is fifteen. (That's normal too.)

Invading Italy made no sense for Charles VIII. Marrying Lisa Gherardini makes no sense for Francesco del Giocondo.

But thanks to the senseless choices of both men, the *Mona Lisa* is now a glimmer on the horizon.

WHAT DOES LISA SEE IN FRANCESCO?

Does she see her ticket out of the convent? Does she see anything at all?

Whatever Lisa thinks, it doesn't matter in Renaissance Florence. Women are powerless. This is not an exaggeration: a woman in Florence needs a male guardian to approve almost any decision she makes outside the home. There are a few women who carve out space for their own lives, but they are rare exceptions, and even they exist in a world created and controlled by men. The world of Renaissance Florence is a vast preserve of male power. Even Nannina de' Medici—the sister of Lorenzo himself, as privileged as a woman in Florence could be— famously remarked, "O do not be born a woman if you want your own way."

The irony is overwhelming. The *Mona Lisa* may be the most visible painting in the world, but Lisa Gherardini herself is almost invisible. For many years, scholars denied that Lisa was the *Mona Lisa* at all. She wasn't important enough, they said. More prominent women were put forward as candidates. Even now, some people claim that the real *Mona Lisa* isn't Lisa at all.

Lisa Gherardini has been erased from her own story. She is like nearly every other woman in the Renaissance.

The story of women in the Renaissance is the story of people doing their best with a set of very bad choices. Even women like Lisa, women lucky enough to marry profitable silk merchants, labor through astonishingly rigid lives. This is a (partial) list of what they could *not* do:

> Own a house
> Own anything at all
> Live on their own
> Go to college
> Have a business
> Enter a government building

Women are not just cut off from participating in public life. They are often cut off from being *in public.* This sort of isolation continues for generations. "In Florence, women are more enclosed than in any other part of Italy," a traveler would remark a full century after the *Mona Lisa* was painted. "They see the world only from the small openings in their windows."

A woman like Lisa has almost no life outside of her home.

All her responsibilities are inside it: Manage the servants. Devote yourself to your family. Do not stray outside this small world.

⌐○

A YEAR AFTER HER WEDDING, LISA GIVES BIRTH TO A SON. SOON ENOUGH, there's a full household of noisy little Florentines. It's around this time that Francesco starts asking around for a painter.

Francesco needs something to hang on the walls of his beautiful home. What would be better than a portrait of his wife, who has given him this family?

It's not hard for Francesco to find a painter. He's surrounded by them.

Florence is insanely rich in an artistic talent, and *insanely rich* is an understatement. It's impossible to convey how much talent there is in this small town. But try this. Imagine a circle with a radius of a few hundred yards—less than a thousand feet—with Francesco's house at the center. Inside that circle are the homes of Raphael, Michelangelo, Botticelli—and the list of luminaries goes on. There may be no place with a greater density of artistic genius in the history of the world.

From this embarrassment of riches, Francesco manages to pick a painter who's sick of painting.

FLORENCE, 1500

B ACK IN FLORENCE, LEONARDO DA VINCI SPENDS HIS TIME NOT ACCEPTING commissions but fending them off.

On his journey from Milan, he stayed with a wealthy noblewoman named Isabella d'Este. He sketched her. Now she wants a painting from him. He could paint her, she says—that would be fantastic—but he could also paint anything or anyone else.

She's a prominent patron. It's an ideal commission, with complete freedom.

Leonardo turns her down. He doesn't feel like it.

Isabella d'Este pesters a friar in Florence who knows Leonardo. The friar writes back: "Leonardo's life is extremely irregular and haphazard, and he seems to live from day to day. . . . He devotes much of his time to geometry, and has no fondness at all for the paintbrush."

Isabella does not take no for an answer. She writes again.

The friar apologizes: "In short, his mathematical experiments have distracted him so much from painting that he cannot abide the paintbrush."

No fondness at all for the paintbrush. Cannot abide the paintbrush.

Perhaps the most gifted artist of his time—a time that includes the most gifted artists of all time—cannot be bothered to paint.

Instead of painting, Leonardo goes in a different direction. A very different direction. He finds arguably the worst person in all of Renaissance Italy—the worst person on a very long list of extremely bad people—and signs up to work for him.

Cesare Borgia is a high-ranking Catholic official and the son of a future pope. But he is not a humble, religious man. He is a monster. He's greedy, cruel, remorseless; he killed his own brother. He's a man who chops up his enemies and leaves their bloody remains in public as a message. A man who, when someone speaks up against him, has that person's tongue and hand cut off and then puts the cut-off tongue inside the cut-off hand and hangs them out a church window as a warning.

Leonardo dislikes violence and cruelty so much that he's a vegetarian—rare at the time. He's known to be gentle and generous. Why would he go to work for an absolute monster?

The answer is simple: he wants the job.

Leonardo is fascinated by engineering and by the technology of war. His notebooks brim with ideas for massive projects. Borgia offers him the opportunity to bring these large sketches to life. Leonardo is unable to resist—this is work he could never do on his own.

He never does it with Borgia either. The only thing he

accomplishes is an entirely new sort of map—the city of Imola as seen from above, drawn in perfect proportion. It's beautiful and stunningly accurate, a major leap forward.

It is also the only thing beautiful about this period. Leonardo follows along as Borgia's army annihilates the countryside. There is blood. There is torture.

Finally, Leonardo comes to his senses: he leaves Borgia.

Back in Florence, he hears from a silk merchant who wants a portrait of his wife. And in 1503, Leonardo, after turning down far more prestigious commissions, after expressing little interest in painting at all, says yes to Francesco del Giocondo.

No one knows why.

If Leonardo met Lisa before he took the commission—we don't know whether he did—maybe he saw something in her. Something that took him beyond financial calculations.

Or maybe not.

Why this woman?

It ranks among the greatest mysteries in the history of art.

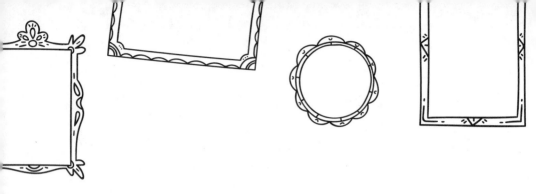

WHY THIS PAINTING?

LEONARDO WRITES A LITTLE BIT OF EVERYTHING IN HIS NOTEBOOKS—
Latin verbs, bad jokes, grocery lists. But in all the notebooks,
there's nothing about the *Mona Lisa.*

Nothing. No contract, no sketches, no correspondence. Nothing about why he agreed to do the painting. Nothing about what he was trying to do with the painting.

Nothing at all.

We know the *Mona Lisa* shouldn't have existed. Its existence is an improbable series of improbable events. But we know little about how it defied those odds—how it came to be.

We do know that Lisa sat for her portrait somewhere in Florence. She likely sat for a few days, but it could have been weeks. People said later that there were musicians in the room to entertain Lisa, to make her smile. But people like to make up stories about famous paintings, and the musician story is a good story. In the long history of the *Mona Lisa,* people will make up a lot of good stories, and they will often make the mistake of believing them.

Instead of answers, we have questions. Why did Leonardo take so long to paint the portrait? Some scholars claim he never finished it. Why did he become obsessed with perfecting it? It was his least remarkable commission—no job seemed less promising. Why did he focus all his skill and imagination on this diminutive portrait of a wife and mother?

To answer these questions, all we have is the *Mona Lisa* itself. It is stubbornly silent. Its eyes follow you around the room, but its mouth never moves.

If we look closely, though, we can see something new. We can look past its fame and see how *strange* the painting is.

On her wooden board, Lisa Gherardini is no longer in Italy. She's been transplanted into some science-fiction world, where there are no humans or any signs of any humans, except a random bridge. Far below her, mountains rise and streams flow, but this isn't the Italian countryside. It isn't anywhere people live. It's strange even by the standards of strange Renaissance backgrounds.

Now look at Lisa herself. Her face turns toward the viewer, but her body faces away, as if she's just turned—as if she's *still* turning. This makes her look in motion, like she wasn't expecting to be in this painting at all. Her hands face us, but they're empty; she holds nothing. That's strange. In Renaissance art, paintings are littered with things standing in for other things. Everything is symbolic. There's nothing symbolic in the *Mona Lisa,* because there's nothing there to symbolize anything. Lisa wears plain clothing and no jewelry, and that's strange too. Florentine men and women knew how to dress: even their everyday clothing was extravagant. But Leonardo puts Lisa in as ordinary an outfit as possible. She doesn't even look important enough to be in a painting.

But she acts like she belongs there. She's not shy or meek. She makes eye contact. This is exactly how Florentine women are taught *not* to behave, and it is also how Leonardo himself taught not to paint them. He wrote that women should be painted with "their heads lowered and inclined to one side." But he does the exact opposite.

Lisa Gherardini herself lived in a world of strict social codes. Her behavior was carefully controlled. She couldn't break the rules. But in his portrait of her, Leonardo could and does.

This is the irony of the *Mona Lisa*. It's a painting that breaks all the rules—but it is of a woman who could break none.

⌒

STILL, THE QUESTION LINGERS. WHY IS IT SO FAMOUS? WHY IS IT THE MOST famous painting in the world?

Why this painting?

Some say it is because the painting is uniquely *open*. They mean you can interpret it any way you like. The *Mona Lisa* doesn't mean anything on its own, so every generation can invent its own *Mona Lisa*. Every generation can find its own meaning.

Maybe that's part of it.

Other people talk about the technical details. Leonardo coated the wooden panel with an extra thick layer of white lead paint. Then he laid countless thin layers of paint on top. He understood that light would pass through the thin layers and bounce off the white lead. The base would reflect the light, sending it back out again.

Parts of the *Mona Lisa* seem to glow. This is why. The painting is generating its own light.

That might be part of it too.

Some people talk about the technical magnificence of the painting—how Leonardo took everything he'd learned about the world and put it all on this piece of poplar wood. The *Mona Lisa* is the height of sfumato. It's all blurred edges and smoke, without a single visible brushstroke.

But it isn't the only technically magnificent painting in the world. Not by a long shot.

Still other people talk about the *Mona Lisa phenomenon*. This is the spooky way in which Lisa's eyes follow the viewer around the room. Wherever you are, she's already there, looking at you. That's true—but you can see the same effect in other portraits. Leonardo was especially good at it, yes, but that isn't why people notice it.

They notice it because they're looking so closely. It's the *Mona Lisa* phenomenon only because we've bothered to notice it in the *Mona Lisa*.

Finally, a lot of people will say the *Mona Lisa* is famous for her mysterious smile. It's a smile that looks less like a smile if you look at it and more like a smile if you look away. That's definitely part of its fame too. But no one talked much about the smile until recently.

Why is the *Mona Lisa* the most famous painting in the world?

The best reason has nothing to do with Leonardo da Vinci.

The best reason has to do with a man in a white smock who once spent the night in a closet.

Before 1911, the *Mona Lisa* was an exquisite painting. Among a small number of people, it even had a small amount of fame. But it wasn't *popular*.

It was the theft that made the *Mona Lisa* a celebrity.

In order to stay famous, though, the painting needed the limelight. It needed to stay on the front page and in the public eye. Being stolen briefly is a great career move. Being stolen forever is a career killer.

So it was very good news that at the end of August of 1911, the Paris police already had the thieves in sight.

A WILD AND PERFECT PAIR

IN WHICH LOUIS LÉPINE FINDS AN INTERNATIONAL GANG OF THIEVES AND A MONKEY

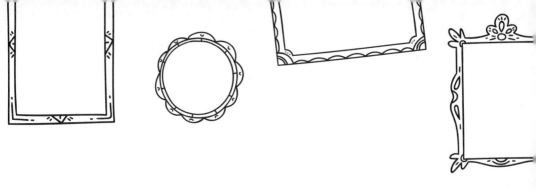

A STATUE STOLEN FROM
THE LOUVRE

O N AUGUST 29, 1911, A HEADLINE IN THE *PARIS-JOURNAL* SENT THE *MONA Lisa* investigation straight off a cliff:

A THIEF BRINGS US A STATUE STOLEN FROM THE LOUVRE

Below was a sensational letter the *Paris-Journal* had just received, with a few identifying details omitted:

Monsieur,

On the 7th of May, 1911, I stole a Phoenician statuette from one of the galleries of the Louvre. I am holding this at your disposition, in return for the sum of _____ francs. Trusting that you will respect my confidence, I shall be glad to meet you at [such and such a] place, between _____ and _____ o'clock.

The *Mona Lisa* theft was the best story in Paris, and anything stolen from the Louvre was potentially connected. Was the *Paris-Journal* willing to pay for stolen goods to get closer to that story?

The *Paris-Journal* was absolutely willing to do that. A reporter met with the young man who'd sent the letter—the paper described him as having "a kind heart and a certain lack of scruple." The newspaper put its newly acquired statue in its front window, and hundreds of Parisians showed up to see it. The offices of the *Paris-Journal* briefly became an extremely small satellite of the Louvre.

Embarrassingly, the Louvre hadn't even known the statue was missing. Until the statue showed up on the front page, the museum hadn't noticed it was gone.

It was a spectacular story for the *Paris-Journal*. They'd recovered stolen property. They'd humiliated the Louvre. They were potentially on the trail of the *Mona Lisa,* the hottest story of the new century. But it wasn't enough. For any newspaper in Paris, the question was always: How do we keep the story going? How we sell the paper *tomorrow*? So the *Paris-Journal* assigned the thief to tell his own story. His escapades, it turned out, had begun years before:

It was in March, 1907 that I entered the Louvre for the first time—a young man with time to kill and no money to spend. . . . It was about one o'clock. . . . A single guard was sitting motionless. I was about to climb the stairs leading to the floor above when I noticed a half-open door on my left. . . .

The thief finds himself in a small gallery, by himself.

It was at that moment that I suddenly realized how easy it would be to pick up and take away almost any object of moderate size. . . . Being absolutely alone, and hearing no sounds whatever, I took the time to examine about fifty heads that were there, and I chose one of a woman, with, as I recall, twisted, conical forms on each side. I put the statue under my arm, pulled up the collar of my overcoat with my left hand, and calmly walked out, asking my way of the guard, who was still completely motionless. . . .

I sold the statue to a Parisian painter friend of mine. He gave me a little money—fifty francs, I think, which I lost the same night in a billiard parlor.

The thief said he went back the next day and stole another statue, and when he returned to Paris after a long absence, in May 1911, he helped himself to another. But since the *Mona Lisa* was stolen, he complained, everything had changed: "I shall probably have to wait several years before resuming my activities."

To the Paris police, it was an extremely promising lead: a thief who stole from the Louvre *and* a Parisian painter who bought stolen goods. The *Paris-Journal* hinted that these men might have stolen the *Mona Lisa* too.

A hunt was soon underway for the thief the *Paris-Journal* had met with—a young Belgian named Géry Pieret. He was

a small-time crook. But he was connected to people who were anything but small-time—including a painter who was about to become the most important artist of this new century.

This meant the hunt for the thief would have very strange consequences. The *Mona Lisa* was the height of Renaissance art. But its theft sparked a series of events that would threaten to derail the highest achievements of *modern* art.

For a few weeks in 1911, the future of painting itself hung in the balance.

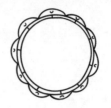

THE ESTEEMED
WILHELM ALBERT WŁODZIMIERZ
APOLINARY KOSTROWICKI

THE UNSTOPPABLE RISE OF THE *MONA LISA* IS A CENTURIES-LONG SAGA.
There are a lot of stories along the way. But there is no story sadder than that of Guillaume Apollinaire.

Which is a shame, because before the *Mona Lisa* is stolen, there was no one happier.

Guillaume Apollinaire has the best name in this story, but his full name is even better, a magnificent mouthful: Wilhelm Albert Włodzimierz Apolinary Kostrowicki.

He was born in Rome to a Polish mother from extremely, extremely minor nobility. His father was Swiss. His grandfather was Russian. He was a melting pot of European nationalities in a single wool suit.

Apollinaire claimed to have a high aristocratic background—he also claimed his father was a cardinal or a pope—but if so, there was no money left. As a child, his family would slip out of hotels in the middle of the night, leaving the bill behind.

After a childhood of moving around, Apollinaire arrived in

Paris as a young man and immediately felt at home. He found his voice in poetry, the new modernist variety. His poetry was dazzling and intimidating, but Apollinaire himself was soft and affectionate. He became a sort of mascot in Montmartre, his seedy, beloved neighborhood. Everyone who knew Apollinaire loved him, and almost everyone knew him.

It helped that if you saw him once, you knew him for life. He had a face like a cartoon, or a massive stone head, or a Roman emperor who'd eaten too many pastries. His mouth was tiny and his eyebrows were like commas, little flicks on his forehead. He loved wandering around Paris. He did his best writing while walking, ideally while also talking. These were his hobbies: walking and talking.

"Guillaume was extraordinarily brilliant," said the American writer Gertrude Stein, who knew everyone on the Parisian scene, "and no matter what subject was started, if he knew anything about it or not, he quickly saw the whole meaning of the thing and elaborated it by his wit and fancy carrying it further than anybody knowing anything about it could have done, and oddly enough generally correctly."

Gertrude Stein knew Apollinaire best in the company of a young, fiery Spaniard—you could call him Apollinaire's Parisian painter friend.

That's what the Paris police would call him.

⌐—ᵒ

PABLO PICASSO WAS MADE FOR THIS REVOLUTIONARY NEW CENTURY, AND HE arrived in Paris right on time: 1900.

Short and intense, with eyes that burned, the Spanish painter could not talk like Apollinaire. His French was a work in progress for years. But he could paint like no one else, and soon, he would make his name painting like no one had before.

Wearing grubby blue overalls, the uniform of an electrician, Picasso slept by day and worked by night, with a smoldering sort of discipline. In his early years in Paris, he lived in total poverty. It was not by choice. It was because almost no one wanted his paintings.

His Montmartre apartment, which doubled as his studio, was tiny. Its walls were barely thicker than tissues. In the winter, the apartment was freezing—there was only a single stove for warmth, with a mountain of ashes beside it. In the summer, the rooms were so hot they were unbearable. Visitors wore next to nothing.

Picasso's studio was unfit for polite society and, maybe because of that, it became an unlikely salon. It was a loud, intoxicating place. Guests stopped by constantly, trying to make sense of this new world he was putting down on canvas. Dogs scampered through the mess. So did Picasso's pet mouse. So did Picasso's pet monkey.

Picasso himself was magnetic. He wasn't smooth or well spoken. In fact, he was explosive. But he had the future of painting inside him.

That future was called *cubism*. It required nothing less than tearing up all the rules of perspective. That was no small thing. Perspective—making a flat surface appear to have depth— was the great achievement of Renaissance painting. It was the innovation that made possible all the paintings hanging in the Salon Carré. But Picasso didn't want to paint from *a* perspective. He wanted to paint from *every* perspective: to paint each side of a person or a thing all at once.

With unbelievable nerve, Picasso, along with Georges Braque, a housepainter turned modernist painter, eliminated almost all color and perspective from their work. What was left was shape: every shape seen from every angle all at once. It was high-risk art. *We were like mountain climbers roped together,* Braque said later.

Their work was shocking and confrontational. Looking at it required *effort*. Even Braque thought they might have gone too far. Before he joined with Picasso, he criticized cubism as too aggressive. He compared the process to drinking kerosene in order to spit fire: the effect would be magnificent, but you'd die in the process.

Braque was both wrong and right.

They didn't die.

But the effect *was* magnificent.

⌒

PICASSO CHALKED A GREETING ON HIS FRONT DOOR: *AU RENDEZ-VOUS DES poètes.*

It didn't say *Meeting place of painters.* The painters who visited Picasso's studio mostly left bewildered. It said *Meeting place of poets.* It was the poets, not the painters, who understood what Picasso was trying to do, and the principal poet of Picasso's circle was Apollinaire.

They were a perfect pair: Picasso couldn't talk, but he could paint like no one else; Apollinaire couldn't paint, but he could talk like no one else. Together, they completed each other. Their fame rose in tandem.

But that fame was very fragile.

TWO STATUES AND A PISTOL

BORN IN BELGIUM, GÉRY PIERET FOUND HIS WAY TO PARIS AT A YOUNG age. Charming and handsome, with a bent for crime, he met Guillaume Apollinaire while both were working for an investment magazine called *Le Guide des Rentiers*. Having Apollinaire give investment advice may sound like a horrible idea, and it was. The authorities shut down the magazine, either for failing to advise investors correctly or for succeeding in advising investors incorrectly.

Apollinaire had grown fond of Pieret. He gave him a splendid new name—Baron Ignace d'Ormesan—and put him in his stories. He also hired him as his occasional secretary. After the magazine failed, when Pieret was briefly homeless, Apollinaire let the young Belgian crash on his couch.

It was the worst decision Apollinaire ever made.

On a fateful day in 1907, Pieret got up off the couch and told Marie Laurencin, a painter and Apollinaire's partner, that he was going to the Louvre that afternoon. "Can I bring you anything you need?" he asked her politely.

The Louvre wasn't just a museum. It was also the nickname for a department store, the Grands Magasins du Louvre. Marie Laurencin figured that Pieret was going shopping.

And he was, sort of. He just wasn't intending to pay. That evening, he returned to Apollinaire's apartment with a stone head from the Louvre—the museum, not the department store. Then he went back the next day and did it all over again.

Sculptures in the Louvre were not locked down or behind glass. They sat on tables, unsecured, like objects in someone's living room. They saw few visitors who weren't lost. But Pieret's stolen sculptures had a more exciting life in front of them. They would upend the *Mona Lisa* investigation—and they would change the course of modern art.

Not bad for a couple of ancient stone heads no one wanted.

⌒◦

WELL, *ALMOST* NO ONE.

Pablo Picasso wanted the sculptures, and he bought them from Pieret. They rhymed with his ideas. In fact, they looked like they'd been made by an early cubist—a very, *very* early cubist. The connection was uncanny.

Picasso was about to make a major advance in his art—a leap so far forward that few would appreciate what he was trying to do. The statues helped him make that leap; they provided half the inspiration he needed. The other half he discovered in the

Musée d'Ethnographie du Trocadéro. If the Louvre was full of objects bought or stolen from throughout Europe, the Trocadéro was full of objects bought or stolen from everywhere else. France had a vast colonial empire: at the turn of the twentieth century, it stretched across almost all of west and central Africa. It was a violent, racist endeavor, and the French stripped their colonies of anything they found remarkable or valuable. These objects often ended up in Paris, and once in Paris, they often ended up in the Trocadéro.

The museum was a dusty, moldy, underfunded, neglected mess. It was supposed to be educational, a record of different peoples and cultures. (It did not educate anyone about colonialism or how the objects on display got there.) It was not supposed to contain anything as grand as art.

But Picasso did not care. When Picasso went to the Trocadéro, he knew the significance of what he was looking at: "I understood why I was a painter." He stocked his head full of what he saw.

The masks he visited there were from what is today the country of Gabon, on the west coast of Africa. In the Trocadéro, they were presented as ageless, unchanging, primitive objects, evidence of an ageless, unchanging, primitive culture. Those were the assumptions made by the Parisian curators, at least, and they were all wrong. The masks Picasso saw—expressive, sharply featured, wholly new—were in fact recent works of art, and they were brilliantly innovative.

Picasso seized on those innovations. He went home, stretched an enormous canvas—eight feet by eight feet—and set to work on a painting that became known as *Les Demoiselles d'Avignon.*

There are rare moments in history when a single object or action changes everything—when there's a clean, violent break with the past and a tumble into an uncertain future. In the history of modern art, that honor belongs to *Les Demoiselles d'Avignon.*

It's a painting of a small group of women—the subject wasn't new. But Picasso has abandoned any sense of perspective, and the effect is shocking. For centuries, painters tried all sorts of tricks with perspective to make paintings look like they weren't flat. Picasso doesn't use any of these tricks. *Les Demoiselles d'Avignon* looks extremely flat. Picasso's tricks are different: He wants to show his subjects from multiple angles all at once. A squatting figure, for example, is shown from all angles simultaneously—back, front, side.

The figures on the right are inspired by the African masks. The figures on the left are taken straight from Pieret's statues. A half century later, Picasso admitted this: "If you look at the ears of *Les Demoiselles d'Avignon,* you'll recognize the ears of those sculptures!"

Today, art historians like to say that *Les Demoiselles* empowers viewers, which is what they say about the *Mona Lisa* too—they mean that both paintings are open to interpretation. But the similarity ends there. If the *Mona Lisa* is the most famous human face in art history, *Les Demoiselles* is a hatchet thrown at it. It's not a pretty painting. It's brutal and uncomfortable.

At the time, no one felt empowered by *Les Demoiselles.* They did feel something, though: they felt like they hated it. Visitor after visitor walked through Picasso's studio and stared at *Les Demoiselles* in disbelief. A blank wall would have received more compliments.

In a decade, Pablo Picasso would be famous. But fame had not yet arrived. Picasso lived in a decrepit apartment, and he'd painted a massive work no one could stomach. He rolled up *Les Demoiselles* and stashed it away. (It wouldn't appear in public for another thirty years.)

Still, Picasso believed in his vision, and he believed that the future would vindicate him.

He was right.

But he almost never got there.

He was almost destroyed by the statues that inspired him.

⁓

LIKE ANY SENSIBLE PARISIAN, PABLO PICASSO WAS NOT IN PARIS IN AUGUST of 1911.

He'd fled the heat for the cool air of the countryside. Picasso got out of Paris every summer, and this time he'd rented a house in the Pyrenees, the mountain range between France and Spain. There were few comforts; it was as far from modern life as you could get in France. For Picasso, it was perfect.

Then disaster struck: the *Paris-Journal* arrived in the Pyrenees, with Pieret's account of his theft on the front page. Picasso read it with increasing horror. In Paris, Apollinaire had the same reaction.

They had good reason to be horrified. There were statues Pieret hadn't returned, and Picasso and Apollinaire knew where those statues were. They also knew Pieret. They knew him well enough to know that they had no idea what else he might have done. He might have stolen the *Mona Lisa* itself. Even if he hadn't done it, he'd surely be suspected of it.

The stolen statues, the suspicious connection with a known thief: it was enough to ruin Picasso and Apollinaire.

The pair were insiders in Montmartre but outsiders elsewhere in France. They were poor, and they were immigrants. They worked on the edges, making art that few people understood or liked. They were far from the establishment, far from anyone who could protect them. And they were connected to people who wanted to overthrow that establishment: anarchists.

The core belief of anarchism is that government is oppressive and that people will be free only when they can govern themselves directly. At the time of the theft of the *Mona Lisa*, anarchism in France had a violent tinge. Less than twenty years before, an anarchist had assassinated the French president. Bombings were not uncommon. The threat of violent anarchism stalked the French state.

Picasso and Apollinaire were close to some anarchists, and the government knew it. Deep in the archives of the Paris police is Picasso's file: his friends, his questionable associations, his political leanings. (What it says exactly is still a secret.) There's surely an entry on the anarchist playwright Alfred Jarry, who once gave Picasso a Browning pistol—the gun favored by the anarchists. It was a joke. Picasso was supposed to use the pistol to go to war against the old traditions of art. Picasso found the pistol useful. When asked what a painting meant, he often fired it. It was a very persuasive form of art criticism.

But the police might look at that pistol and see a very different sort of war.

Picasso packed up his things in the Pyrenees. He left his monkey with the neighbors. He raced back to Paris.

He was about to change the course of art history—and he knew it.

He just had to stay out of jail.

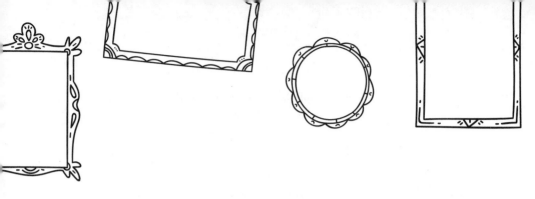

DR. NO
(PART 2)

HY WERE PICASSO AND APOLLINAIRE SO WORRIED?

Let's return to the stolen statues.

Géry Pieret thought the statues were Phoenician, made by the sea people of ancient Greece. They were not. They were Iberian, made by the people who'd lived in Spain before the Romans. They came from Picasso's homeland, the south of Spain.

Picasso was a great collector, and he loved to collect Spanish art. He especially loved neglected pieces, the cast-offs of art history. He was a magpie, and his studio was a junkyard of shiny objects, where everything was on display.

But not the Iberian heads.

Picasso had a reason to hide the heads: he knew exactly where they were from. In fact, he knew their specific section of the Louvre extremely well. He was said to stalk the exhibits there, to pace "around like a hound in search of game." Picasso knew he owned stolen property. He could hardly deny it. The statues were stamped on their bottom:

PROPERTY OF THE MUSÉE DU LOUVRE

But Picasso's involvement went deeper than simply buying the statues.

Imagine Pieret, walking into the Louvre. The security is atrocious. He has his pick of the collection. Why does he choose these heads?

Not to sell. At the time, there was no market for this kind of ancient statue.

Not for fun. The heads were heavy and awkward; they were difficult to steal.

Not for himself. Remember, Pieret doesn't even know *what* he's stolen—he thinks the heads are Phoenician, not Iberian.

That leaves a couple of choices:

1. Pieret happened to pick an object that was impossible to sell, tricky to steal, and specifically desired by Picasso. This is possible. It's extremely unlikely, but it is possible.

Or:

2. Pieret was told where to go. Pieret was told what to steal.

It seems a lot more likely that the statues were a commissioned theft. They were stolen for a very particular collector, who wanted to enjoy them in the privacy of his own home. There *is* a Dr. No in this story, it turns out. It's Pablo Picasso.

He doesn't have a mansion. He has a decrepit Montmartre apartment.

Picasso was so worried because he was guilty. To an art critic, the evidence was right there on canvas—all the Paris police had to do was look at the *Les Demoiselles d'Avignon*.

Or, in case the Paris police weren't art critics, they just had to open Picasso's dresser.

The heads, all wrapped up, were at the back of his sock drawer.

PICASSO HAD RUSHED BACK TO PARIS WHEN HE READ THE BAD NEWS IN THE *Paris-Journal*. There he found Apollinaire, who had worse news: He'd just seen Pieret. In fact, Pieret had been staying at his place when the *Mona Lisa* was stolen. When Apollinaire heard about the heist, he'd wondered if his houseguest might be connected. Even if he wasn't, the young Belgian was clearly capable of trouble, and Apollinaire got nervous: he gave Pieret money and sent him out of town.

This meant that Apollinaire was guilty of helping a fugitive escape. And if Pieret *had* stolen the *Mona Lisa,* Apollinaire was guilty of aiding the most wanted man in the world.

Picasso and Apollinaire considered fleeing France. But they still had the statues, and like the gun in a murder, the statues tied them to the theft. They needed to dump them as soon as possible.

What would a murderer do with a gun? He'd throw it in a river. So Picasso and Apollinaire decided to throw the statues into the Seine. But the statues were more conspicuous than a gun, and what if someone saw them fall into the Seine? They changed their plan. They decided to put the statues in a suitcase and throw the *suitcase* into the Seine.

At Picasso's apartment that night, the two played cards. They never played cards; they knew nothing about playing cards. They were *acting*. What would bandits do before they went out on a job? Picasso and Apollinaire figured bandits would play cards. Therefore, they, too, would play cards.

At midnight, they left Picasso's apartment with a heavy suitcase. Paris was quiet, but noises echoed through the cobblestoned streets. Shadows rose up out of nowhere. In every shadow, they saw a policeman. "They thought they were being followed," said Fernande Olivier, Picasso's partner, who'd just watched them fail to play cards. "Their imagination conjured up a thousand possibilities," she added, "each more fantastic than the last."

The reality was bad enough.

The painter and the poet finally returned to Picasso's apartment in the middle of the night. They were still carrying the suitcase. Either they were too scared to toss the statues, or they couldn't stomach the thought of them at the bottom of the Seine. In any case, they were terrible bandits.

They were also exhausted. For the last time, they went to sleep alongside the ancient Iberian heads.

In the morning, Apollinaire picked up the suitcase and went for another walk. He didn't walk to the Seine. He walked to the *Paris-Journal*.

⌒＿＿つ

THE *PARIS-JOURNAL* COULDN'T BELIEVE ITS LUCK. ITS BANNER HEADLINE RAN:

WHILE AWAITING MONA LISA *THE LOUVRE RECOVERS ITS TREASURES*

By taking the statues to the *Paris-Journal,* Apollinaire had done Picasso a huge favor: he'd let his friend stay out of the story. The newspaper promised not to reveal Apollinaire's name, but the promise was hollow. Everyone there knew Apollinaire. (He'd written for the *Paris-Journal* himself.) His identity was certain to leak.

Apollinaire told the newspaper he'd seen its photograph of Pieret's statue and was shocked—*shocked*—to realize that his ancient heads might also have been stolen from the Louvre. He'd had no clue. But once he suspected they were stolen property, he'd brought them in immediately.

It was all a lie, of course. It was not a lie that would last.

In August of 1911, any stolen property from the Louvre was potentially connected to the *Mona Lisa* theft, and with the Paris police eager to make an arrest, no one was going to think too hard about how strong that connection was. Being connected to the statues was bad enough for Apollinaire. But then Géry Pieret, being Géry Pieret, made everything worse.

The following day, the *Paris-Journal* printed a letter from "our thief" about the worst possible subject: the *Mona Lisa*. "I hope with all my heart that the *Mona Lisa* will be returned to you," Pieret wrote. "I am not counting very heavily on such an event." Pieret urged the portrait's thief not to sell the painting but to confide in the *Paris-Journal*. "I can only urge the person at present holding Vinci's masterpiece to place him entirely in your hands. He has a colleague's word for it that your good faith is above all suspicion."

It did not sound like the letter of an innocent man. It sounded like the letter of a man who knew a lot more than he was saying. Pieret might as well have written to the Paris police and said: *By the way, I know a lot about the* Mona Lisa *theft. You might want to investigate everyone I know.*

Which was exactly what they did.

THE ENEMY WITHIN

THE KNOCK AT APOLLINAIRE'S DOOR CAME LESS THAN A DAY LATER.

Apollinaire opened it to find a pair of detectives on his doorstep. They turned Apollinaire's apartment upside down, and somewhere in the chaos, they discovered letters from Géry Pieret.

It was enough. Apollinaire was taken downtown to the Palais de Justice. He confessed that he knew Pieret and that he'd helped him leave Paris. Since Pieret was now a fugitive from justice, Apollinaire was arrested and charged with harboring a criminal and helping him flee.

But the Paris police suspected that Apollinaire's involvement went far beyond that.

"We are on the trail of a gang of international thieves who came to France for the purpose of despoiling our museums," a police spokesman announced. "Monsieur Guillaume Apollinaire committed the error of giving shelter to one of these criminals. Was he aware of what he was doing? That is what we are to determine. In any case, we feel sure that we shall shortly be in possession of all the secrets of the international gang."

The international gang.

An international gang of thieves had finally been found, and according to the logic of the investigation, if there was an international gang, the *Mona Lisa* couldn't be far behind. Languishing in jail, still wearing his wool suit, Apollinaire was charged with the theft of the *Mona Lisa*.

France was still haunted by the Dreyfus affair—the idea of the enemy within. Unlike Dreyfus, Apollinaire was not Jewish, but the antisemitic publications of the day simply called him Jewish. He *was* an immigrant—he'd adopted France and loved it unabashedly, but he was now cast as a foreigner. In the popular press, Apollinaire was no longer a poet or an art critic. He was no longer a representative of French culture. He was the enemy within.

Louis Lépine paid Apollinaire a visit in prison.

Apollinaire had no choice. He talked.

THE NEXT KNOCK WAS AT PICASSO'S DOOR.

It came early, around seven in the morning. For Picasso, who rarely got up before noon, it was an obscene hour. He stumbled to the door in his bathrobe and found a detective standing there.

Picasso was expected at the Palais de Justice, the detective told him. He was expected in court *now.* He should get dressed.

The painter, fearless in his art, walked back to the bedroom, shaking with fright. He was trembling so much he couldn't even dress himself; Olivier had to help him. Picasso picked out a red-and-white polka-dotted shirt and a clashing tie. It was a statement of defiance, like a matador dressing for the bull ring.

He did not look like a matador, though. He looked ridiculous.

While Picasso was on his way downtown, Apollinaire sat in a small holding cell at the Palais de Justice. He was dirty, exhausted, pale. His collar was ripped; his tie was gone. He must have thought he'd sunk as low as he could go. He was about to sink lower.

After hours in the smothering cell, Apollinaire was led past a crowd of photographers and into a courtroom. The whole world was watching him, the first person arrested in the theft of the *Mona Lisa*. "I found myself suddenly stared at like a strange beast," Apollinaire wrote later. "I think that I must have laughed and wept at the same time."

Picasso looked at him and saw a stranger—he'd never seen the dapper, dignified poet look like this. If they could do this to Apollinaire, what could they do to him?

Picasso was terrified and desperate to save himself. When the judge asked if he knew the puffy, pathetic man across the courtroom, Picasso looked carefully at his friend.

"I have never seen him before," he told the judge.

For Apollinaire, this was worse than everything that had come before—worse than the arrest, the photographers, the humiliation. In his hour of greatest need, his closest friend had pretended not to know him. He'd been abandoned.

In court, Apollinaire admitted that he'd owned stolen art from the Louvre. He admitted that he'd sheltered Pieret and enabled his escape. He even admitted that, years ago, he'd signed a manifesto that called for the Louvre to be burned to the ground. But he did not admit to stealing the *Mona Lisa*—he hadn't stolen it, after all. Picasso admitted guilt and denied it by turns. What exactly he said—how much he betrayed his friend—is still unclear. Neither Picasso nor Apollinaire were reliable witnesses to their own lives.

But to the Paris police, a single disappointing truth was becoming clear: these men did not look anything like an international gang of thieves—or at least not one that was capable of stealing the *Mona Lisa*. Ultimately, the police had no evidence tying the pair to the heist. Louis Lépine's case was falling apart. The *Mona Lisa* looked further away than ever.

Picasso was released but ordered to stay in Paris. The painter was shattered. His immense self-confidence—the audacity that had allowed him to invent a wholly new style of painting—was gone. He stayed indoors, leaving his apartment only at night, switching taxis to elude anyone following him. He expected to be arrested at any moment.

He'd survived, but it would be a long time before he believed it.

THE MAN WHO HAD STOLEN
THE *MONA LISA*

AFTER ALMOST A WEEK IN THE LA SANTÉ PRISON, GUILLAUME APOLLINAIRE walked free.

He did not go home. He went to the offices of the *Paris-Journal,* the very place where the story had begun, and wrote a lengthy account of his time in jail. "I had an impression of death," he said of entering prison. "I felt that I was now in some place beyond the bounds of the earth, where I would be utterly lost."

The charges against him had not been dismissed, and they hung over his head for months. Like Picasso, he assumed he'd be arrested again. He was deeply depressed and unnerved by every knock. His reputation was stained. Even his partner, Marie Laurencin, ignored him.

Most of all, he feared deportation from France, and for good reason: he was now associated by name with the theft of the most famous painting in the world. Almost half a century later, a friend of his would write: "Guillaume Apollinaire abruptly became famous throughout the entire world. He was thought of as the man who had stolen the *Mona Lisa*. Even today there are Parisians who believe it, and who are a little disappointed to learn that Apollinaire had nothing to do with the theft."

The whole episode, the *"affaire des statuettes,"* would hang over his head for the rest of his short life.

The "impression of death" Apollinaire had felt upon entering prison—it was not wrong.

⌒‿つ

BACK AT THE PALAIS DE JUSTICE, LOUIS LÉPINE WAS STILL LOOKING FOR HIS international gang of thieves. *La bande de Picasso*—the Picasso gang—had checked almost every box. It was international. It was a gang. And it included thieves.

They just hadn't stolen the *Mona Lisa*.

Louis Lépine had come so close to what he was searching for. He was nowhere near where he needed to be.

A DANGEROUS WOMAN

IN WHICH LEONARDO LEAVES THIS WORLD AND THE *MONA LISA* BECOMES MYSTERIOUS

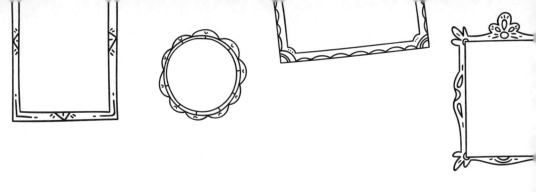

ROME, 1513

I T IS NOW A DECADE SINCE LEONARDO DA VINCI BEGAN THE *MONA LISA.*

Does Lisa Gherardini have her portrait? She does not. Has Leonardo finished her portrait? He has not. Will he finish it? No one knows.

Leonardo is now in Rome, where a new pope from the Medici family—Pope Leo X—is busy bankrupting the Vatican by commissioning massive new works of art. There's money in Rome. There's opportunity.

The decision to move was made even easier by the death of Ser Piero di Antonio, Leonardo's father. At the end of his long life, Ser Piero did not forget how Leonardo came into the world: He cut his illegitimate son out of his will. Leonardo inherited nothing.

Leonardo da Vinci is known at the most prominent courts in Renaissance Italy. He has seen sights of unimaginable splendor; he has helped create that splendor. But he's still an outsider, even within his own family.

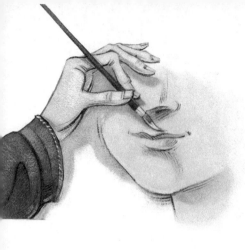

In Rome, Leonardo's commission does not go well: before starting, he decides he needs to perfect the varnish—the thing he'll need after he's *finished* painting. Pope Leo X observes this and famously says, "Alas, this man will never do anything, because he is already thinking of the end before he has even begun the work."

Instead of the pope's commission, Leonardo works on the portrait he still hasn't given to Francesco and Lisa Gherardini. He adds invisible brushstroke after invisible brushstroke. He takes everything he's learned about painting since he arrived in Verrocchio's studio and focuses it all on Lisa Gherardini.

Even incomplete, the *Mona Lisa* is considered a masterpiece by other artists at the time. Raphael, the young prodigy of Renaissance painting, is so entranced that he makes his own versions. Leonardo still isn't finished, though. He won't let the painting go.

The *Mona Lisa* isn't all Leonardo is working on, of course. He studies the manufacturing of mirrors, a diabolically difficult business. He proposes an elaborate drainage system for the Roman marshes.

And he cuts up bodies in the dead of the night.

⌒୨

LEONARDO HAD DISSECTED HIS FIRST CADAVER DECADES BEFORE. IT QUICKLY became an obsession. In a single Florence winter, he once dissected twenty bodies.

His notes from the dissection sessions are exhaustive. His drawings are astonishing. The sketches make you feel as if you're looking into the cadaver alongside Leonardo—that this body has been opened up in front of *you.*

Imagine him there in the hospital. There's no refrigeration, so a human body is rotting in front of him. The corpse smells, and with every passing minute, it smells more. The scent of death soaks into Leonardo's robes. Flies circle his head.

To Leonardo, it is irresistible. The next night, or the next week, there's another body. He does it all over again.

Leonardo is frank about the difficulties. In order to outline all the veins, he has to use several bodies in succession, because "a single body would not last long enough"; it decays so fast it becomes unusable. "You will perhaps be deterred by the rising of your stomach," he writes.

The veins, the spine, the nervous system: it is all there in Leonardo's notebooks, immaculately crosshatched and detailed. He is especially fascinated by the heart. At the time, the heart was thought to be a sideshow, a second-rate organ. People believed that the liver controlled blood circulation. In contrast, Leonardo saw that the heart was at the center of things—at the *heart* of things. But he saw this because he trusted only his own observations; he wasn't blinded by his expectations. Even more remarkably, Leonardo deduced the way valves of a beating heart open and close— something he *couldn't* have seen. (A stopped heart doesn't beat.) It wasn't until the 1960s that medicine finally agreed with him.

During the day in Rome, Leonardo works on the *Mona Lisa*. During the night, he traces the inner workings of a person alive only hours before. These activities are intimately linked. Leonardo's anatomical adventures teach him how faces are put together. His sublime portraits are partly the product of his time with ravenous flies and rotting bodies. To look at the *Mona Lisa* is to see Leonardo in the morgue, a flayed face in front of him, tracing the nerves and muscles that come together to make a smile.

Word of his midnight activities gets out. "The pope has found out that I have skinned three corpses," Leonardo writes in his notebook. It's a serious offense. Dissection is forbidden by the Roman Catholic Church. It's heretical—against the word of God.

He gets off easy. He's simply told: *Please stop skinning corpses.* For once, he listens.

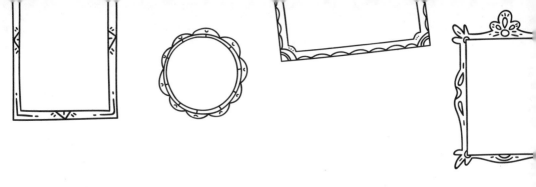

FRANCE, 1516

WHILE LEONARDO IS IN ROME, SKINNING CORPSES, FRANCIS I PASSES through town.

The young, buoyant king of France is an intellectual, and a man of tremendous energy and curiosity. He's a perfect match for Leonardo. Francis recruits Leonardo to join his court at the Château d'Amboise, in the Loire Valley.

Leonardo has never been to France; he knows no one there. He's sixty-four, an age few people reach at the time. He's never left Italy, and leaving now might mean never returning.

But he accepts. Maybe he's desperate. Maybe he feels undervalued. Maybe a new adventure promises new knowledge.

On the longest journey of his life, Leonardo crosses the Alps. It's summer. The wildflowers are out. Snow sits only on the highest peaks. The *Mona Lisa* crosses with him, on the back of a mule.

In France, Leonardo's only obligation is to talk to Francis about whatever Francis wants to talk about. For the first time in his life, Leonardo has a patron who adores him. Francis calls Leonardo a "philosopher-magician." He later says that he "could never believe there was another man born in this world who knew as much as Leonardo." At the very end of a life spent searching for a home, Leonardo has finally found a place of his own—very far from his native Italy.

Only a few years into this comfortable semi-retirement, Leonardo runs out of time. He is sixty-six when he writes the final entry in his final notebook.

It is said that Francis himself is at Leonardo's deathbed.

AFTER LEONARDO'S DEATH, THE *MONA LISA* IS INHERITED BY A LONGTIME assistant and then purchased by Francis. It begins a long life spent inside stuffy French buildings.

It hangs in a royal bathroom—a really fancy bathroom, but still, a bathroom. It's nearly traded away to England. Its reputation declines. When the Louvre is founded after the French Revolution at the end of the 1700s, the *Mona Lisa* isn't considered the finest Renaissance painting in the collection. It isn't even close to the finest. The Louvre values the *Mona Lisa* at far less than another Leonardo, his *Virgin of the Rocks,* and both are valued at a fraction of the works of Raphael.

The *Mona Lisa* was on its way to obscurity.

It had already had a very full, very improbable, very strange existence. It was painted by a man who didn't want to paint

anymore; it was painted of a woman who almost wasn't around to be seen. It was a modest portrait that for a time became the highest refinement of Renaissance painting.

But by the 1800s, the *Mona Lisa* was seemingly destined to be just another extraordinary Renaissance painting in a museum of extraordinary Renaissance paintings. It would be a small, bewitching rectangle on the wall, drawing an occasional glance, not crowds.

Instead of this placid fate, the story of the *Mona Lisa* gets really peculiar. There's yet another twist in a story that's already very twisted.

Instead of sliding into obscurity, the *Mona Lisa* becomes a temptress.

She becomes a dangerous woman. A mysterious woman. The woman we know today.

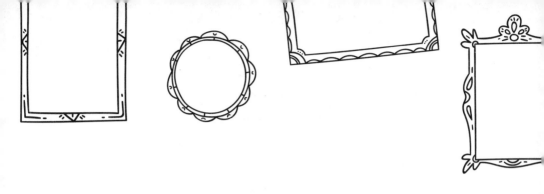

PARIS,
1850

HER TRANSFORMATION BEGINS WITH A SINGLE MAN, THE FRENCH POET
and critic Théophile Gautier.

In mid-nineteenth-century France, Gautier is a hugely influential writer. He's also a mess, and he's especially a mess around women. Like many men of his era, he has trouble seeing women as real people. He's more comfortable with women as *ideas,* and he's most comfortable imposing his ideas on them. For Gautier, women are contradictions: gentle and manipulative, hot and cold, heaven and hell.

When he looks at the *Mona Lisa,* he sees the same contradictory mix, and it intimidates him. Standing before this portrait, he writes, you feel like "a schoolboy before a duchess." Above all, Gautier is enthralled with her expression, which "attracts you irresistibly and intoxicates you." But he's also disturbed by it; it mocks you, he writes. "The arc of her lips," he adds elsewhere, "appears to be about to erupt into divine sarcasm, heavenly irony, angelic derision."

(This is just how Gautier writes.)

Gautier could have written this about almost any painting—he was haunted by dozens. But he picked the *Mona Lisa,* and that made all the difference. His ode to it changes its story, because Gautier is obsessed with a facial feature that no one else has dwelled on:

Her smile.

Gautier makes the *Mona Lisa* into a figure of mystery. No one has called the *Mona Lisa*'s smile mysterious for hundreds of years. But after reading Gautier, *everyone* sees a mystery there.

Suddenly, her smile—no longer cheerful, now enigmatic—is the key to the whole painting.

Other people—all men—begin to see the *Mona Lisa* the same way. "Beware, *La Gioconda* is a dangerous picture," writes the French historian Jules Michelet. "The painting attracts me, revolts me, consumes me." An artist leaps to his death and blames the *Mona Lisa:* "For years I have grappled desperately with her smile," he writes in a suicide note. "I prefer to die."

When Lisa Gherardini sat for Leonardo, she was powerless. She couldn't even choose her own husband. Now, hundreds of years later, her portrait is powerful enough to lure men to their deaths.

The *Mona Lisa* becomes an icon of the Romantic age. For the Romantics, love drives you crazy, and the *Mona Lisa* represents the highest form of insanity. The English critic Walter Pater manages to outdo even Gautier with an over-the-top description that begins: "She is older than the rocks among which she sits; like the vampire, she has been dead many times, and learned the secrets of the grave; and has been a diver in deep seas, and keeps their fallen day about her; and trafficked for strange webs with . . ."

Pater's sentence goes on and on, and then on some more, finally stopping some fifty words later. It becomes legendary. A generation of English schoolboys will quote it by heart.

The Irish writer Oscar Wilde later says that when he looked at the *Mona Lisa,* he didn't see the painting: he saw Pater's description. The beauty of an artwork doesn't belong to the artwork itself, Wilde says. It belongs to the critic, who decides what it means. Anyone can walk into the Louvre and see a painting. A good critic can look at the painting and tell you what you *don't* see. A good critic can find things whether they're there or not. That's what Gautier and Pater did.

Before they came along, the *Mona Lisa* was "a portrait of a certain merchant's wife in a cheerful mood," as one historian put it. By the time Gautier and Pater were done, the *Mona Lisa* has been transformed. It's no longer good-natured or innocent. It's mysterious, alluring, unknowable. It's a puzzle of a portrait.

The way we see the *Mona Lisa* today was laid out by a few obsessed men 150 years ago.

Still, the portrait isn't famous yet. Going to look at art is an elite pastime—this is long before crowds flock to museums. Few people know anything about art, and even fewer know the name of a single painting.

For the *Mona Lisa* to break out of this elite circle, something dramatic would have to happen. Something that would make it less of an artwork and more of an icon. Something that would put it on the front page.

The very last improbable event of all.

MY NAME IS LEONARD

IN WHICH A MAN WITH A BLACK HANDLEBAR MUSTACHE WALKS INTO AN ART GALLERY

THERE IS NO GROUND TO HOPE

N PARIS, THE AUGUST HEAT HAD PASSED. AN AUTUMNAL CHILL HAD AR-
rived. The investigation had gone cold too: after the flurry
of excitement over Guillaume Apollinaire, there were no new
arrests.

With nothing new to report, the *Mona Lisa* could not hold
the front page forever, and it was finally booted off by an *actual*
gang of thieves. The Bonnot Gang was a group of anarchists
who were more criminal than political. They robbed. They
murdered. They invented the getaway car.

It was a sensational story, and the only thing that could
knock it off the front page would be the sinking of the *Titanic.*

Which was exactly what happened next.

The *Mona Lisa* was left in its dead wake.

By 1913, the portrait had disappeared from the papers and
the Louvre: it was no longer listed in the museum catalog. After
four hundred years in France, the *Mona Lisa* had left for good.
The official investigation was closed, and a devastating verdict

was issued: "There is no ground to hope that *Mona Lisa* will ever resume her place in the Louvre."

The *Mona Lisa* was replaced by a Raphael, a portrait of a man named Baldassare Castiglione. This was appropriate: Raphael had paid tribute to the *Mona Lisa* by painting his own versions, and his Castiglione was also turned to the side. It was a great painting—it is perhaps the greatest Renaissance male portrait—but Baldassare Castiglione would never be a celebrity.

After a very long life spent in public, the *Mona Lisa* was living out her days in private.

Soon, surely, she would be forgotten.

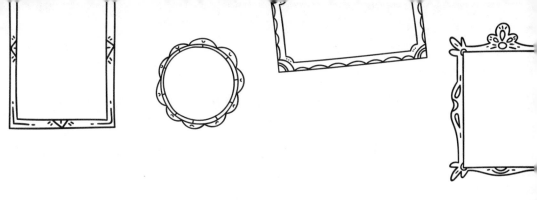

LEONARD

ALFREDO GERI ALMOST THREW OUT THE LETTER.

In fairness, Alfredo Geri got a lot of mail. A prosperous art dealer in Florence, Geri advertised in newspapers across Europe, looking for art and antiquities. That November morning in 1913, he scanned the mail to see what he'd been offered. It wasn't much.

Then he opened the last letter.

It was from a self-proclaimed Italian patriot, now living abroad in Paris. The writer—he signed the letter Leonard—complained that the Louvre was filled with loot Napoleon had taken from Italy. Many of France's treasures were actually Italy's, the writer said, and now it was time for the trade in stolen goods to go the other way. He had the *Mona Lisa,* and he'd like to return it to Italy.

But he needed Geri's help.

Geri laughed. He showed the letter to a friend. They laughed. The letter was impossible to take seriously. The *Mona Lisa* had been gone for years, and during that period, countless people had claimed to have the painting. Just a couple of months before, an English gentleman had nearly fooled the Louvre with a perfectly aged copy. It was almost a rule at this point: anyone claiming to have the *Mona Lisa* was either deeply confused or running a scam.

Geri was about to toss the letter in the trash—but he stopped himself. He checked the envelope: it was postmarked in Paris. He reread the letter. He thought, *Well,* maybe—*if there's a chance . . .*

He conferred with Giovanni Poggi, the director of the Uffizi, the great Florence art museum. Poggi had an esteemed career: he would stay the Uffizi's director for some forty years; he would save the museum's paintings from Nazi looting during World War II. But his obituaries would lead with what happened after Alfredo Geri visited him that November afternoon.

Poggi studied the letter. He was even more skeptical than Geri, but everything was worth trying. Tell this Leonard to bring the painting to Florence, he told Geri. It was almost certainly a copy, so Poggi would have to examine it in person.

Leonard agreed, then canceled. Then he agreed and canceled again.

Then, out of nowhere, Geri got a telegram: it was Leonard; he'd be in Florence the very next day. This time, he showed up. He wore a suit and tie; he had a black handlebar mustache; he had no painting. Geri took him to his office and lowered the shades.

Leonard got straight to the point. The painting was at his hotel in Florence, and it was indeed the *Mona Lisa*. There was no doubt. Leonard could be certain it was the *Mona Lisa* for a very simple reason: he'd stolen the painting himself.

Geri, so skeptical before, was intrigued. But he had a problem—a major problem. Leonard had shown up so suddenly that Poggi was out of town. He wouldn't be in Florence until the next day. And without Poggi, Geri couldn't be sure whether this *Mona Lisa* was a fake or not.

He stalled. Either he offered a reward or Leonard asked for a reward—accounts would differ—but in any case, Geri had no intention of paying anything. He just wanted to get his hands on the painting, and he'd say almost anything to make that happen.

Geri explained that he needed the director of the Uffizi to authenticate the painting. Could Leonard come back the next day?

Leonard agreed to return—but would he? He'd just admitted to stealing the *Mona Lisa*. If he did, Geri might be waiting for him with the police. Why would he trust Geri? Why would he show up again?

And if he didn't, the *Mona Lisa*—if it *was* the *Mona Lisa*—would vanish once again.

The following day, Geri and Poggi waited for Leonard.

And waited. And waited. Leonard was late.

Finally, Poggi put on his coat to leave—and Leonard walked in.

A MANGLED HAT,
A MANDOLIN

THE UNLIKELY TRIO WENT OFF TO MEET THE *MONA LISA*.

Leonard wasn't nervous, or at least he didn't act nervous. He acted like a tourist. It was his first time in Florence, and anyone watching him would have thought he'd gone there to see the sights. There was a lot to see. At its core, Florence is a small city, and the trio were walking down the same streets Leonardo and Lisa had walked down. They passed by buildings Leonardo and Lisa must have known, stone walls they must have touched. Florence is a town thick with time.

Eventually, they arrived at a place that neither Leonardo nor Lisa ever knew: the Hotel Tripoli-Italia. Leonard had taken a cramped room on a top floor, room #20. The three of them could barely fit in it together. It wasn't clear where there was space for the *Mona Lisa* too.

Leonard locked the door and pulled a trunk out from under the bed.

Geri later made a list of what Leonard took out of it:

Broken shoes
Another pair of shoes
A mangled hat
A pair of pliers
Tools for plastering
A smock
Paintbrushes
A mandolin

It was a pile of "wretched objects," Geri said. And—and that was it. The trunk was empty. Poggi and Geri could see the bottom. It had all been for nothing. There was no *Mona Lisa*.

But then Leonard took out the bottom of the trunk—it had been a false bottom. And there, lying on the real bottom, was a rectangular object, wrapped in a red silk cloth.

Leonard placed the silken bundle on the bed, next to the mangled hat and the mandolin. He said nothing.

In the small room, with scarcely enough room to stand, there must have been scarcely enough air to breathe.

Leonard began to unwrap the red silk. And then, according to Geri: "To our astonished eyes, the divine *Gioconda* appeared, intact and marvelously preserved. We took it to the window to compare it with the photograph we had brought with us. Poggi examined it and there was no doubt that it was the original. The Louvre's catalog number and stamp on the back of it matched with the photograph."

They'd found the most valuable painting in the world in a cheap hotel.

Years of false leads, years of international intrigue: it was all over.

Almost.

Because now they had another task: they had to steal a painting from a thief.

Poggi was already convinced it was the *Mona Lisa,* but he did not tell Leonard that. He said it *appeared* to be the portrait, but they'd need to be absolutely sure. To confirm its authenticity, they'd have to take the painting to the Uffizi. Leonard, still serene, agreed.

On their way out of the Hotel Tripoli-Italia, the three were stopped by the hotel's concierge, who accused them of having a stolen painting.

This was awkward, because it was true.

But the concierge didn't mean a painting stolen from the Louvre. He meant a painting stolen from the Hotel Tripoli-Italia. He thought they were walking out the door with one of *his* paintings.

If the Louvre's security had been as good, the *Mona Lisa* would never have been stolen.

~~~⌁~~~

THE TRIP TO THE UFFIZI MUST HAVE BEEN EVEN MORE STRESSFUL THAN THE walk to the Hotel Tripoli-Italia.

Before, Alfredo Geri and Giovanni Poggi thought they had a lead on the *Mona Lisa.* But the odds were against it. The odds were always in favor of a scam.

Now they were confident they had the *Mona Lisa*—and they were carrying it through a crowded city. They had no protection. A thief could have bumped into the group and made off with the portrait.

Even worse, they were accompanied *by* a thief.

In his Uffizi office, Poggi double-locked the door. He compared the painting with photographs of the many cracks, or craquelure, in the original. Every old painting has countless cracks, the marks of age. A gifted forger can copy a painting, but he cannot copy a craquelure. Like a fingerprint, every craquelure is unique.

The cracks were identical.

Now they just had to talk Leonard into leaving behind the most valuable painting in the world.

The *Mona Lisa* simply wasn't secure at the Hotel Tripoli-Italia, Poggi told Leonard. They'd have to keep it at the Uffizi; the museum was the safest place for it.

On the one hand, this was clearly true. On the other hand, it was a bizarre thing to tell a thief. Of course, the portrait wasn't safe with Leonard. Even Leonard knew it wasn't safe with him. He'd stolen it!

But Leonard didn't object. Maybe he was swayed by Poggi's status—he'd been impressed that the director of the Uffizi was meeting with him. In any case, he agreed to leave the painting, and Poggi told him they'd be in touch tomorrow.

He was lying.

They'd be in touch a lot sooner.

An hour later, the Florence police knocked on room #20 of the Hotel Tripoli-Italia.

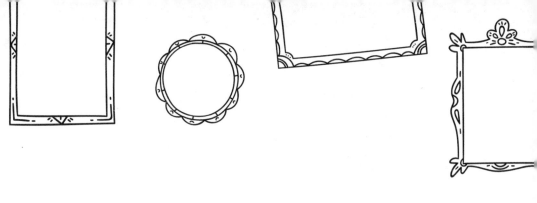

A HOUSEPAINTER

IN PARIS THAT EVENING, A PHONE CALL INTERRUPTED A LOUVRE CURATOR at dinner.

No, the curator told the caller. *It's impossible.* He hung up and went back to his dessert. Someone was trying to fool him into thinking the *Mona Lisa* had been recovered. He wasn't going to fall for it.

In 1911, no one could believe the *Mona Lisa* had been stolen.

In 1913, no one could believe the *Mona Lisa* had been found.

But as unlikely as it was, as impossible as it seemed, it was true.

A parade of experts arrived at the Uffizi to examine the portrait. No one disagreed with Giovanni Poggi. Even the skeptical French finally admitted it was the real thing. "I only wish that the French would consider it a copy," the Italian art historian Corrado Ricci said. "Then *Mona Lisa* would remain in Italy."

When the news broke, it stopped an actual fistfight among legislators on the floor of the Italian Parliament. *"La Gioconda ha trovato,"* a legislator shouted. *The* Mona Lisa *has been found.* The fight was forgotten.

The *Mona Lisa* had come back to its birthplace. All of Italy rejoiced.

Like a dog who travels across the country to find its owners, the *Mona Lisa* had somehow found its way home. Instead of in the United States, or in Germany, or at the bottom of the Atlantic, the portrait had turned up only a few blocks from where it was painted. The Tripoli-Italia was practically next door to the building where Lisa likely sat for Leonardo.

It felt as if the painting had brought the thief to Florence, rather than the other way around.

⌒୨

THE FIRST THING LEONARD TOLD THE POLICE WAS: *MY NAME ISN'T LEONARD. It's Vincenzo Perugia.*

Just over thirty years old, Vincenzo Perugia had left Italy for France when he was still young. It wasn't by choice, and he wasn't alone: massive unemployment in Italy had pushed many Italians to emigrate. Perugia found work painting houses in Paris. He wasn't getting rich. When he was arrested, the police found less than a couple of francs in his wallet—the equivalent of ten dollars today.

He also had the most valuable painting in the world, of course. But just *having* it wasn't worth anything. He'd had it for over two years and he hadn't made a cent.

Perugia confessed almost immediately. Yes, he'd stolen the

Mona Lisa, he told the Italian police, but that didn't make him a thief.

It made him a hero.

That explained why he'd come back to Geri's gallery even though he'd admitted to the theft. It explained why he'd returned to his room at the Tripoli-Italia even though the police would know where to find him. It explained why he'd made zero effort to cover his tracks.

He believed he had nothing to fear.

He believed he was a hero—the man who'd brought the *Mona Lisa* home.

Everyone had guessed wrong. The thief wasn't a Secret Admirer. It wasn't a Lone Madman. It wasn't a Consummate Professional or a Rich American.

Vincenzo Perugia was a new character: the Patriotic Italian.

⇛

THE STORY PERUGIA TOLD THE POLICE BEGAN A YEAR BEFORE THE THEFT, when the Louvre decided to put its most famous paintings behind glass.

Because the glass was controversial, it had to be as invisible as possible. The Louvre hired a firm that specialized in glazing, the art of glass fitting and sizing, but even these skilled workmen had to redo the job multiple times before the curators were satisfied. In the process, the crew learned exactly how the Louvre hung and protected its paintings. It was valuable inside information, but it meant absolutely nothing to almost everyone on the crew.

Except a man named Vincenzo Perugia.

The theft of the *Mona Lisa* is full of ironies, but this is the most ironic of them all: if the Louvre had never bothered to put the *Mona Lisa* behind glass—if the Louvre had never bothered to protect its paintings—its thief never would have come in contact with it.

Louis Béroud, the painter who'd discovered the *Mona Lisa* missing, had been right all along: The glass wasn't the solution. The glass was the problem.

Perugia would soon leave the glazing firm, but he'd gotten to know the workers at the Louvre and he still visited the museum. As he walked through its Italian collection, he told the Florence police, he marveled at the scale of Napoleon's plunder.

Perugia had only been twelve when he'd left home. In France, he'd been mocked and called anti-Italian slurs. Now he imagined a new future for himself: He would return to Italy with the *Mona Lisa*. It would be a triumphant homecoming for both. "I would be unworthy of Italy," he said, "if I did not return to her one of her masterpieces."

Vincenzo Perugia put the *Mona Lisa* under glass in January 1911. Then he waited.

In August, the Louvre would be half-dead.

The theft itself was simple, he explained: the closet, the white smock, the stairwell. (The only hiccup was the doorknob.) Once he was out the front gate, he simply escorted the *Mona Lisa* home. His apartment was less than a couple of miles from the Louvre, and no one noticed a man carrying a package wrapped in a white cloth. The streets of Paris were filled with far stranger things.

No mansion awaited the *Mona Lisa.* No lair. No Dr. No.

Perugia's apartment was a single furnished room that was barely furnished. The Tripoli-Italia was a step up. Perugia slid the *Mona Lisa* into an opening in the wall and piled firewood in front of it. It would stay there until he moved it to the trunk: the false bottom was built to match the *Mona Lisa*'s measurements.

Louis Lépine's international dragnet—the trains stopped in Belgium, the *Kaiser Wilhelm II* searched in New York—had been for nothing. Pilu, the fortune-teller's dog, had been right all along. The *Mona Lisa* was still in Paris.

No one had a clue, because Perugia hadn't talked. His neighbors had no idea they were sleeping next to the most famous woman in the world. When Perugia's friends visited, he didn't show off the portrait. He played the mandolin.

To decorate his run-down room, Perugia put a postcard of the *Mona Lisa* on the mantel.

Even the man with the actual *Mona Lisa* had a *Mona Lisa* postcard on display.

⌒〜๑

ONCE ITALIANS HEARD PERUGIA'S STORY, MANY AGREED WITH HIM: HE *WAS* a hero.

In jail, Perugia was showered with gifts: wine, cheese, cigarettes. Supporters sent him lunch and dinner daily; someone gave him the equivalent of a couple of thousand dollars. Finally, he'd made something from the theft—he'd just had to go to prison to do it.

Vincenzo Perugia became, briefly, a luminary on the level of the *Mona Lisa* itself. His few possessions were treated like the bones of a saint. People offered huge sums for his mandolin, his paintbrushes, his plastering tools. They even bid for his rags.

Perugia was now a celebrity, but he was still in prison, and he couldn't understand why.

"I have rendered outstanding service to Italy," he complained. "I have given the country back a treasure of inestimable worth, and instead of being thankful, they throw me in jail. It's the height of ingratitude."

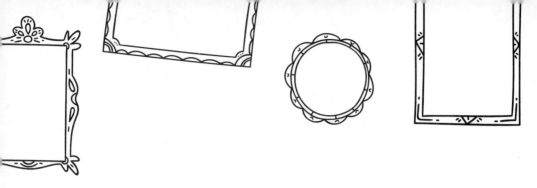

NO WORD SPOKEN
BUT GIOCONDA

THE *MONA LISA* WAS BACK.

The story—the theft, the recovery, the noble thief—once again sold newspapers across the world. There were special supplements and extra editions. The Paris newspaper *Excelsior* even ran a comic-strip-like depiction of Perugia's account—a how-he-did-it illustration of the theft.

In Italy, the appetite was insatiable. "No word is spoken but 'Gioconda,'" the Rome *Tribune* wrote. "Nothing is sought but 'Gioconda.'" A wave of patriotism swept across the country. Maybe Vincenzo Perugia was nuts; maybe he was even a little dim-witted. But he'd stolen the *Mona Lisa* for Italy! The least Italy could do was keep it. Napoleon had stolen it *from* Italy. The theft was an act of justice!

This righteous story was complicated by the fact that it was . . . well, not true. Napoleon, who'd stolen so much else, *hadn't* stolen the *Mona Lisa*—Leonardo himself had taken it to France. The Italian government rejected the cries of many to keep the portrait. "Although the masterpiece is dear to all Italians as one of the best productions of the genius of their race," it announced, "we will willingly return it to its foster country."

Soon.

First, they'd have some fun: The *Mona Lisa* would have a whirlwind tour around Italy—a trip through cities the portrait last saw some four hundred years before. It would be the first traveling blockbuster art exhibition in history. For a few cold gray weeks, all of Italy was lit up by the *Mona Lisa*.

The first morning of the tour, over thirty thousand Italians gathered outside the Uffizi, waiting for the doors to open. The crowd grew restless. Windows were broken. The Uffizi staff rushed to move busts and sculptures before they were trampled. The *Mona Lisa* was in more danger than it had been in Perugia's apartment.

In the presence of the portrait, men removed their hats. Soldiers saluted. Elderly women crossed themselves—Lisa Gherardini had become a religious icon. "Oh, it is she, it is she," a visitor cried. "The lost is found."

After a few days in Florence, the *Mona Lisa* traveled to Rome in style. It had come from France on the cheapest ticket. Now it had a private train car, an armed guard, and a padded case made out of rosewood.

The portrait spent a couple of nights in Rome, where it was painted. It was not enough time, and after the final night, the police were called to disperse the many people who still wanted to see the painting. In Milan, where *The Last Supper* was peeling off the wall, the crowds to view the *Mona Lisa* were reported to be sixty thousand. On the painting's last night there—possibly

the last night it will ever spend on Italian soil—the exhibition stayed open until midnight.

The *Mona Lisa* arrived in Paris to cheers and jubilation. At the Louvre, well over one hundred thousand visitors filed past the portrait in the first forty-eight hours. It broke the attendance record; it buried the attendance record.

The painting had returned to the Louvre almost undamaged. But it had changed anyway; it was not the same portrait that had been stolen. The *Mona Lisa,* in its time away, had grown to be monumental, almost mythical. Parisians flocked to the Louvre to see it, but the real *Mona Lisa* was in their heads. It was too big, too legendary to fit in any museum.

The *Mona Lisa* had changed so much the Louvre could have changed its wall label. It could have added another name.

Leonardo da Vinci had painted the *Mona Lisa.*

But Vincenzo Perugia had turned it into *the Mona Lisa.*

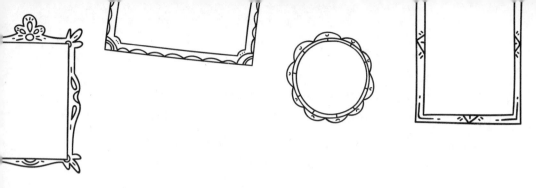

A NOBLE MISTAKE

THE TRIAL OF VINCENZO PERUGIA, WHEN IT FINALLY TOOK PLACE MONTHS later, was hardly a trial at all.

The French never requested that Perugia be returned for trial, and it was unclear whether the Italians had the right to hold one. They did, but the court proceeding was mostly a glorified fact-finding inquiry. The panel of judges asked Perugia the questions everyone wanted answered anyway.

Under scrutiny, his story began to fray. His patriotic luster became tarnished.

The housepainter turned out to have a criminal record. He'd been arrested twice before, once for attempted robbery. More importantly, he'd tried to sell the *Mona Lisa*. In Perugia's notebooks, the authorities found a list of potential buyers, and many weren't Italian. J. P. Morgan was there. So was Henry Duveen, the London dealer who'd been offered the painting.

Duveen's instincts had been right: the man in his gallery did have the *Mona Lisa* after all. Duveen had said nothing to the police at the time, but he had no regrets. "I would sooner have gone around with a stick of dynamite in my pocket for the rest of my life than have had any knowledge of that affair," he said later.

Perugia claimed he'd just wanted "advice" from Duveen on how to take the painting to Italy. Besides, he didn't want the money for himself, he said; he simply wanted to provide his parents with "a comfortable old age."

As the trial went on, Perugia lied in ways that could have been meaningless but could have been purposeful. He claimed he hadn't spent the night in the Louvre, for example, when he clearly had. It didn't make sense. Was he trying to protect anyone who'd helped him? Were there other thieves still out there?

There had to be more to the story.

Perugia eventually confessed that he'd had help from a pair of Italian brothers in Paris, the Lancelottis. The Paris police immediately arrested the brothers. But they said they knew nothing about the *Mona Lisa,* and the police had no evidence against them except the word of a thief. The Lancelottis were let go.

A more exciting development, at least for the newspapers, followed the discovery of some love letters in Perugia's room. An elaborate tale made its way into the press: Perugia had saved the life of a young woman named Mathilde—there was talk of a fight at a dance hall—and they'd fallen in love. Then she was killed, or she succumbed to illness, or, in any case, she died. (The details shifted a lot.) She was gone. But she'd looked strikingly like the *Mona Lisa*—this was the clever twist in the tale—and so Perugia, deep in desperate mourning, had stolen the painting to bring her back to life. The theft was a tribute to their grand, tragic romance.

There was only one problem: it wasn't true. But there was such a strong desire for a better story that many people involved *tried* to make it true.

⌒──○

IF THE TRIAL WAS BAD FOR VINCENZO PERUGIA, IT WAS WORSE FOR THE French authorities.

It revealed that they'd failed to see the person in front of their eyes the whole time. Louis Lépine and Alphonse Bertillon had missed the lesson of the very first detective story: In Edgar Allan Poe's "The Purloined Letter," the suspect hides a scandalous letter in plain sight. No one can find it. It's too visible.

Sometimes it is hardest to see what's most obvious.

There was always strong evidence that the theft was an inside job—whoever had removed the painting had known how it was hung. Who would have known that? The people who'd put the *Mona Lisa* behind glass less than a year before. The glaziers had more intimate contact with the portrait than anyone else in France. A letter to *Le Figaro* had even specifically called for the investigation to focus on the workers who had put the *Mona Lisa* behind glass.

The glass was the central clue, after all. But it wasn't the thumbprint left on the glass. It was the glass itself.

During the early stages of the investigation, the Paris police had written to Perugia, asking him to come in for an interview. It wasn't because they suspected him; they were interviewing everyone who'd worked at the Louvre. Perugia had ignored the letter. A detective finally went to his apartment and questioned him. Perugia claimed he couldn't have stolen the *Mona Lisa*; he said he'd been at work the morning of the theft. But his alibi didn't hold up: Perugia's boss said he'd been late that morning.

Asked about this slip, Perugia said he'd simply slept in. He'd been out late having a good time.

It was at this point—the moment he was caught in a lie—that the investigation lost interest in Vincenzo Perugia. No one asked him any more questions.

The Paris police had been inside the apartment of the thief. They'd come within a few feet of the *Mona Lisa*. They never knew it.

Perugia already had a criminal record. His fingerprints were on file. But Bertillon was loyal to his system, which was searchable by measurements, not fingerprints. If the *Mona Lisa* had been stolen in England, where fingerprints were searchable, Perugia would have been arrested almost immediately. In France, the authorities were helpless. Louis Lépine and Alphonse Bertillon, supposedly the finest detectives in Europe, were far behind the times.

The trial was deeply embarrassing for both men. Vincenzo Perugia had:

1. Put the *Mona Lisa* behind glass.
2. Left a clear print behind.
3. Been missing the morning of the theft.

It was a small mountain of clues. It was a simple theft to solve.

The French police couldn't solve it.

They couldn't solve it because they weren't looking for a housepainter. They were looking for a mastermind; the thief had to live up to the theft. If the *Mona Lisa* had been something else, anything else—a stolen purse, a set of second-rate jewels—the thief would have been found far sooner. Even Perugia knew this was the secret of his success: it hadn't occurred to anyone, he said, that the thief could be a "poor devil" like himself.

Vincenzo Perugia was hidden in plain sight.

Even after the trial, the French authorities still couldn't admit he was guilty. "I do not believe Perugia's story of how he stole the *Mona Lisa*," said a magistrate judge in charge of the investigation. Meanwhile, the Louvre's fired director announced that Perugia had been proven to be "a cunning madman. His misdeed and the preposterous explanation he gives seem to prove it."

The myth was more persuasive than the truth. It was a better story. People will choose the better story every time.

⌒~⌒

AT THE CONCLUSION OF THE TRIAL, VINCENZO PERUGIA'S LAWYER ASKED A simple question:

Who had been harmed by the theft of the *Mona Lisa*?

No one, he said. Everyone had come out ahead. The *Mona*

Lisa hadn't been damaged. The Louvre had gotten its painting back. In fact, it had gotten a *better* painting back: The portrait was now world-famous. People were flocking to see it.

This wouldn't have happened without the work of his client. Sure, Vincenzo Perugia been wrong to steal the *Mona Lisa*. But was it wrong to be a patriotic Italian? He was no thief; he was a man who'd made a mistake, a noble mistake. He'd hurt no one, not even the *Mona Lisa*. The only fair thing was to set him free.

The courtroom cheered. Perugia wept.

It worked. Vincenzo Perugia, the man who'd stolen the most valuable painting in the world—the man who'd sparked a world-wide manhunt—would ultimately be sentenced to the time he'd already spent in prison. He was released to wild applause.

He had good timing. In Europe, there would be very little to applaud for years.

The day after Perugia's release, an anarchist named Gavrilo Princip assassinated the archduke of Austria-Hungary, Franz Ferdinand. The assassination sparked a series of ultimatums and military mobilizations. Tragically, no one backed down, and a month later, World War I had begun. The new technology of this new century—with all its wonder and promise—was now the machinery of death. Europe became a continent of ghosts.

The *Mona Lisa* was recovered just in time. A year later, the portrait might have vanished in the chaos of the war. Even if it had been found, the story of its recovery would have vanished, drowned out by grimmer realities. But before the war, it was a final feel-good story for the world. The wave of publicity cemented the painting as a popular icon.

The *Mona Lisa* sat out World War I, safe in the Louvre.

Its adventure was over. Its thief was found. Its story was written.

THE MARQUIS

UNLESS . . .

Unless it wasn't the real story at all.

Nearly twenty years after the recovery of the *Mona Lisa,* a very different account was published in the *Saturday Evening Post,* the most popular magazine in the United States.

It told the tale the *Mona Lisa* trial had failed to tell. In the trial of Vincenzo Perugia, there was no mastermind. There was no criminal conspiracy. There were no Rich Americans, no Dr. No. Everything that everyone had expected—everything that everyone had wanted—was missing.

But this new story gave everyone what they wanted.

And everyone would fall for it all over again.

Everyone would make the same exact mistakes.

THIS STORY DID NOT FEATURE VINCENZO PERUGIA, A POOR, UNEDUCATED housepainter.

It featured Eduardo de Valfierno.

It was a grand name, and Valfierno lived up to it. He had a head of "leonine" white hair and an air of nobility. He was a minor nobleman, in fact—a marquis. He dressed immaculately; he behaved impeccably.

It was an act. The name was fake. The noble pedigree was fake. But the appearance was good enough to fool anyone, and it did.

Eduardo de Valfierno was an Argentine swindler. He'd done a little of everything, but he specialized in art forgeries. Working with a French forger named Yves Chaudron, Valfierno had conned widows and wealthy men across South America. The two specialized in religious paintings by a Spanish baroque painter named Murillo, and they presented their fakes as stolen Murillo masterpieces. But Valfierno didn't bother to steal the originals. He simply printed up fake newspaper clippings with fake stories about the theft of a Murillo. That was usually enough. If that wasn't enough—if the buyers ever saw the actual Murillo still hanging in a church, for example—Valfierno told them what they'd seen was a copy. You see, he said, the church didn't want to admit that its painting had been stolen. It would have been a scandal. So they replaced it with a clever reproduction.

Everything was topsy-turvy: the originals were fake; the fakes were original.

Best of all for Valfierno, the scheme meant the buyers had no options. They couldn't authenticate the painting, because they knew the painting was stolen. They couldn't sell the painting, because they knew the painting was stolen. The only person they could ask about the painting was Valfierno himself, the person swindling them. It was foolproof, and soon Valfierno and Chaudron left for Europe in search of even wealthier fools to fleece.

Paris was the obvious destination. The obvious prey were the Rich Americans.

Business was good enough in Paris that Valfierno's ambitions grew. His eye wandered to more prominent names than Murillo. He wondered: *Why not sell the* Mona Lisa *itself?*

It was a step up, and it meant a major change in tactics. The *Mona Lisa,* unlike a Murillo, was too well known to vanish without anyone noticing. To sell the *Mona Lisa,* they'd need to actually steal the *Mona Lisa.* They didn't intend to sell the real painting; they intended to sell fakes. But potential buyers would believe their fakes were authentic only if the *Mona Lisa* had really been stolen.

The risk was worth it because Valfierno planned to sell the *Mona Lisa* a half dozen times. Each buyer was an American millionaire, and each would think that he alone possessed the real thing.

There was the small matter of stealing the painting, and for that, Valfierno found an inside source: an Italian housepainter who'd worked in the Louvre. Thanks to him, the heist went off without a hitch. It was, Valfierno said, "the most magnificent single theft in the history of the world."

When news of the theft broke, each American millionaire

believed he was the only one who knew what was *really* happening. The fakes were delivered. The millionaires kept quiet. The whole scheme cleared a stupendous profit.

The only flaw was the housepainter, a man named Vincenzo Perugia. He'd been paid well, but he'd gambled it away, Valfierno said. In a desperate attempt to make money, the housepainter had tried to hawk the real *Mona Lisa*—he'd stolen it from its hideout—to a Florentine art dealer, Alfredo Geri. He'd been caught.

But Eduardo de Valfierno was untouched. Eduardo de Valfierno was rich beyond measure, and he'd pulled off the greatest crime of the century—a work of genius, a work worthy of the *Mona Lisa* itself.

THE *SATURDAY EVENING POST* STORY WAS WRITTEN BY KARL DECKER, A JOURnalist who'd been welcomed at the White House. Over the next ninety years, it has become the foundation of the story of the *Mona Lisa* theft. It has appeared in novels, in films and television shows, in histories of the theft.

It's a wonderful, cinematic story, and there's only a single problem with it.

It isn't true.

Eduardo de Valfierno didn't exist. Yves Chaudron didn't exist.

Karl Decker did exist, though, and he was the least reliable reporter in the United States.

Decker did not report stories so much as *invent* stories. For years, Decker wrote for the newspapers of William Randolph Hearst, and Hearst papers were notoriously loose with the facts. Hearst cared about drama, and Decker was very good at drama. His exploits were notorious. (He once rescued a Cuban revolutionary beauty from prison just before the Spanish-American War broke out. That story was, remarkably, true.)

In his *Saturday Evening Post* article, Decker laid it on thick. The story of how he'd gotten the story was itself a story: he'd known Valfierno for years and had run into him in Casablanca in 1914. Decker described a scene straight out of Hollywood, with scoundrels and swindlers on every corner. His Valfierno was out of the movies too: handsome, dashing, crooked. The story was half detective fiction, half tabloid journalism, and wholly satisfying.

Eduardo de Valfierno and Yves Chaudron have never been identified. None of their flawless forgeries have ever been found. The only evidence for the story is what Decker wrote, and there's no reason to believe what Decker wrote, because he's Karl Decker.

So why did everyone believe it? And why do people continue to believe it today?

Because Decker had taken the best stock stories—the International Gang, the Rich American, Dr. No himself—and he'd pulled them together into a single, spellbinding tale. Decker's story was the story everyone expected. It was the story everyone *wanted*.

It was a relief to finally find it.

In the end, we're all like the French authorities. We're all suckers for a better story.

THE STORY OF EDUARDO DE VALFIERNO HITS CLOSE TO HOME.

We live in a conspiratorial age, and the conspiracy theories about the *Mona Lisa* theft reflect our own time. Many people think that a hidden story is more likely to be the true story—the real story must be the story *beneath* the surface. The biggest problem with these sorts of conspiracy theories isn't that they're untrue, although they often are. It's that they're so hard to *disprove*. Challenge part of a conspiracy theory, and a believer will come up with a new twist that explains what's going on.

In a conspiracy theory, belief matters more than facts. Belief in a conspiracy inevitably leads you away from the facts.

In the *Mona Lisa* theft, we can see this toxic way of thinking in action. The heist wasn't a hard case to solve. But it wasn't solved because a lot of people found conspiracies more credible than evidence. Alphonse Bertillon and Louis Lépine—along with many others—refused to see the evidence in front of them. They were unable to see what they didn't already assume to be true. They believed there had to be a *better* story, a story beneath the surface, a story that required brilliant thieves and brilliant detectives. Even after Lépine and Bertillon failed—even after their failure was exposed—a lot of people decided to repeat their mistakes: they decided to believe in Eduardo de Valfierno.

No one but Vincenzo Perugia believed in a simple house-painter.

THERE IS SOMEONE ELSE WHO MIGHT HAVE BELIEVED IN VINCENZO PERUGIA.

Someone who didn't assume. Someone who observed. Someone whose life was about seeing clearly, without expectations. Someone who didn't already know what he was going to find.

The person who could have solved the theft of the *Mona Lisa* is Leonardo da Vinci himself.

THE AFTERLIFE

IN WHICH VINCENZO PERUGIA OPENS A
PAINT STORE AND LEONARDO DA VINCI EATS
A BOWL OF SOUP

LAST WORDS

THE *MONA LISA* IS THE ONLY SURVIVOR IN THIS STORY. IT HAS SEEN everyone else—so many eras, so many lives—pass before it and disappear out of sight.

DUKE LUDOVICO SFORZA—LEONARDO'S PATRON IN MILAN—WAS CAPTURED less than a year after the French invaded. The French were kind to the duke: he was imprisoned but in luxury. Then the duke tried to escape, and the French were not kind.

Ludovico Sforza, the patron of the lavish Milanese Renaissance, would die, half-mad, in a French dungeon.

THE MALICIOUS CESARE BORGIA SURVIVED ANOTHER HALF DECADE AFTER Leonardo left his employ, a period during which he was poisoned (twice), he was imprisoned (twice), and he escaped (twice). He was also disfigured and exiled from Italy.

But this luck, if it was luck, did not last.

Cesare Borgia would die alone, caught in an ambush in Spain. The knights who attacked him showed no more mercy than Borgia had shown anyone else.

◦───◦

THE FRENCH CRITIC THÉOPHILE GAUTIER WROTE THE GREAT BALLET *GISELLE* and then fell deeply in love with its star ballerina.

She rejected him. So he married her sister.

◦───◦

AT THE DAWN OF WORLD WAR I, GUILLAUME APOLLINAIRE VOLUNTEERED FOR the French army. His loyalty to France had been questioned; now he could prove the doubters wrong.

At the front, a piece of shrapnel flew into his head. Sent back to Paris, Apollinaire was never the same again. His genius had slipped away.

Apollinaire died in the 1918 flu epidemic. The war ended weeks later.

◦───◦

PABLO PICASSO LIVED INTO HIS NINETIES, AND WHEN HE DIED, HIS OBITUARY ran on the front page of newspapers. "The most influential and prolific painter of the 20th century," wrote the New York *Daily News*. "The titan of 20th century art," said the *New York Times*.

But Picasso knew how he'd survived the *Mona Lisa* farce, and only near the end of his long life did he tell the truth about Apollinaire and the *affaire des statuettes:* "When the judge asked me: 'Do you know this gentleman?' I was suddenly terribly frightened, and without knowing what I was saying, I answered: 'I have never seen this man.' I saw Guillaume's expression change. The blood ebbed from his face. I am still ashamed. . . ."

GÉRY PIERET ESCAPED TO CAIRO, WHERE HE FOUND WORK AS AN EDITOR. Things went well until he hosted a formal-dress Christmas party. At the end of the party, the lights mysteriously short-circuited. The guests were less than sober, and they made easy prey for Pieret, who snuck through the darkness and relieved them of their valuables.

He'd triggered the power outage, of course.

It worked the first time. The second time, he was caught.

He wound up in the Belgian army in World War I. Toward the end of the war, he wrote a letter to an acquaintance: "A few days ago, I was sitting by an open window when a raven suddenly flew into the room. I felt I was getting a message from Guillaume Apollinaire. I'm very worried about him and beg you to tell me whether he's still alive."

Apollinaire died the day the letter was received.

ALPHONSE BERTILLON PASSED AWAY THE YEAR AFTER THE *MONA LISA* WAS recovered. He never admitted that he'd been wrong about Alfred Dreyfus.

The Bertillon system died with him. Bertillon had barely been buried before his successor declared that fingerprints were the future.

⌒

BEFORE LOUIS LÉPINE RETIRED, HIS PARIS POLICE TRACKED DOWN THE leader of the Bonnot Gang. Lépine survived the encounter. The leader of the Bonnot Gang did not.

⌒

VINCENZO PERUGIA'S HOMETOWN WELCOMED HIM AS A HERO. HE SERVED IN the Italian Army in World War I and moved back to France after the war. There, he returned to the subject he knew best: he opened a paint store.

⌒

LISA GHERARDINI NEVER SAW HER FINISHED PORTRAIT.

After her husband's death, she entered a convent. She spent her final years there.

She had no inkling of the bizarre afterlife that awaited her.

THE HOTEL TRIPOLI-ITALIA NO LONGER EXISTS. IT IS NOW THE HOTEL LA Gioconda.

Tripadvisor ranks it #398 of 428 hotels in Florence.

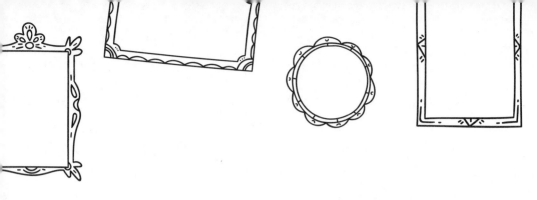

THE SOUP

THE VERY LAST WORDS WE HAVE FROM LEONARDO ARE ON HIS FINAL notebook page.

The page is covered with right triangles. The sides of the triangles all have different lengths: Leonardo is trying to keep the area of a triangle the same and vary the lengths of the sides. It's a geometry problem, and he's not done yet. He needs more time.

It's 1518. He is sixty-six years old.

Suddenly, in the middle of a geometry explanation, he stops.

"*Et cetera,*" he writes.

Then he adds a final note: "*Perché la minesstra si fredda.*"

Because the soup is getting cold.

He would go on, you see, but he has to eat.

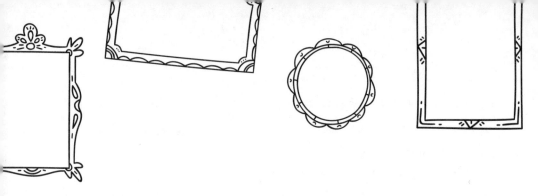

EPILOGUE

IN THE CENTURY SINCE ITS TRIUMPHANT RECOVERY, THE *MONA LISA* HAS only become more famous.

It had already survived four hundred years and a kidnapping when World War I arrived. It survived World War I. It survived World War II. (It was hidden from the Nazis in a series of country estates.) In the last half century alone, it has survived having a rock thrown at it, red paint sprayed at it, and a teacup hurled at it.

Its improbable fame has never been dented.

It is now famous for being famous, which naturally brings it even more fame.

It's the most parodied painting in history, but every parody just draws more attention to the original. When the French artist Marcel Duchamp drew a mustache on a copy of the *Mona Lisa,* he made the most famous parody in art history. But he also made the *Mona Lisa* itself even more famous.

The portrait no longer travels, but when it toured the United

States in the 1960s, it was received like a visiting dignitary. It rode down empty highways in a fireproof, waterproof case, escorted by Secret Service agents. Over a million and a half people went to see the portrait in less than a couple of months. In Tokyo a decade later, there were so many visitors that each was allowed no more than ten seconds in front of the portrait.

It's been hard for the modest *Mona Lisa* to live up to its reputation. When it visited the Soviet Union, the Soviet leader Leonid Brezhnev called Lisa "a plain, sensible-looking woman." In New York, a visitor stared in wonder and said: "It's no bigger than a twenty-one-inch television screen!"

The myth of the *Mona Lisa* is far larger than the *Mona Lisa* itself.

THE *MONA LISA* IS NOW BETTER KNOWN THAN THE LOUVRE. If it were the only painting there, its audience would scarcely be smaller. And each morning, when visitors are let into the museum, they head straight for it. People elbow in to take photos of the most reproduced painting in the world; their photos are worse than the reproductions. They have a few seconds in front of the *Mona Lisa,* and they spend it taking a bad photo.

It is hard to blame them. An audience with the *Mona Lisa* is a brush with fame itself. It's intoxicating.

It's ironic, though: Leonardo is the least appropriate painter for this sort of fame.

Leonardo da Vinci led a life of relentless curiosity. He always wanted to know more. He always wanted to know what he didn't yet know—what no one yet knew.

The crowds in front of the *Mona Lisa*—the parade of tourists behind other tourists—represent the opposite of how Leonardo lived. Today everyone goes to see the *Mona Lisa* precisely *because* they already know the *Mona Lisa*. The smile is supposed to be mysterious, but the painting itself is never a mystery.

It raises a question: Would Leonardo da Vinci go to see his own painting?

Maybe.

Or maybe he'd turn his back on it and observe the crowds instead. Maybe he'd see something new there.

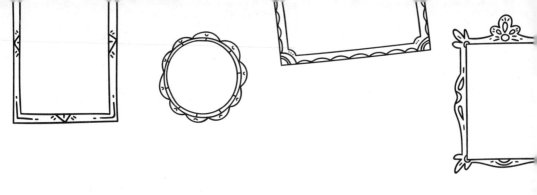

ACKNOWLEDGMENTS

FOR HER FAITH AND UNERRING COUNSEL: MY AGENT, BRENDA BOWEN. IT'S a privilege. And an extraordinary stroke of luck. I am deeply grateful.

For her vision and mysterious ability to improve absolutely everything: my editor, Annie Kelley. Working together has been a dream. (The *good* kind.) Let's do it again soon.

For making these plain words into a work of art: Brett Helquist.

An all-caps thank you to everyone at Random House Studio who worked on these pages. We made a book! For design wizardry: Katrina Damkoehler and Michelle Crowe. For copy-editing, proofreading, and indexing wizardry: Elizabeth Johnson, Jackie Hornberger, and Alison Kolani. And for all-around wizardry: Tisha Paul and Charlotte Roos.

In Buffalo: the University at Buffalo Library, the Buffalo Public Library, Remedy House, Tipico. In Berlin: Staatsbibliothek zu Berlin.

For invaluable feedback: Isaiah Day and Nathaniel Iliff.

With love: Susan and Douglass Day. Madeleine Day and Molly Peterson. Lina Bernstein, David Kramer, Ilya Bernstein. Isaiah, who's read everything but these lines, and Samuel, who was waiting until it was *a real book*. (It was a safe bet at the time.) And Anya. No words (but these).

SOURCES

Amore, Anthony M., and Tom Mashberg. *Stealing Rembrandts: The Untold Stories of Notorious Art Heists.* New York: Palgrave Macmillan, 2012.

Beavan, Colin. *Fingerprints: The Origins of Crime Detection and the Murder Case That Launched Forensic Science.* New York: Hyperion, 2001.

Belting, Hans. *The Invisible Masterpiece.* Chicago: University of Chicago Press, 2016.

Boas, George. "The Mona Lisa in the History of Taste." *Journal of the History of Ideas* 1, no. 2 (1940): 207.

Charney, Noah, ed. *Art and Crime: Exploring the Dark Side of the Art World.* Santa Barbara, CA: Praeger/ABC-CLIO, 2009.

Charney, Noah. *The Thefts of the Mona Lisa: On Stealing the World's Most Famous Painting.* ARCA Publications, 2011.

Clark, Kenneth. *Leonardo da Vinci.* New York: Penguin, 1993.

Cohen, Joshua I. *The "Black Art" Renaissance: African Sculpture and Modernism Across Continents.* Oakland: University of California Press, 2020.

Cole, Simon A. *Suspect Identities: A History of Fingerprinting and Criminal Identification.* Cambridge, MA: Harvard University Press, 2002.

Decker, Karl. "Why and How the Mona Lisa Was Stolen." *Saturday Evening Post,* June 25, 1932.

Duveen, James Henry. *Art Treasures and Intrigue.* Garden City, NY: Doubleday, 1935.

Esterow, Milton. *The Art Stealers.* New York: Macmillan, 1966.

Freundschuh, Aaron. "Crime Stories in the Historical Urban Landscape: Narrating the Theft of the *Mona Lisa.*" *Urban History* 33, no. 2 (2006): 274–92.

Gardner, James. *The Louvre: The Many Lives of the World's Most Famous Museum.* New York: Atlantic Monthly Press, 2020.

Goron, Marie-François. "Number 94," *Pearson's Magazine* 15 (1906): 493–97.

Green, Christopher. *Picasso: Architecture and Vertigo.* New Haven: Yale University Press, 2005.

Green, Christopher, ed. *Picasso's Les Demoiselles d'Avignon.* Cambridge: Cambridge University Press, 2001.

Hales, Dianne. *Mona Lisa: A Life Discovered.* New York: Simon & Schuster, 2014.

Harris, Ruth. *Dreyfus: Politics, Emotion, and the Scandal of the Century.* New York: Henry Holt, 2010.

Hirsch, Alan. *The Duke of Wellington, Kidnapped!* Berkeley: Counterpoint, 2016.

Hoobler, Dorothy, and Thomas Hoobler. *The Crimes of Paris: A True Story of Murder, Theft, and Detection.* New York: Little, Brown: 2009.

Houpt, Simon. *Museum of the Missing: A History of Art Theft.* New York: Sterling, 2006.

Isaacson, Walter. *Leonardo da Vinci.* New York: Simon & Schuster, 2017.

Jones, Jonathan. *The Lost Battles: Leonardo, Michelangelo and the Artistic Duel That Defined the Renaissance.* New York: Knopf, 2012.

Kelly, Joan. "Did Women Have a Renaissance?" In *Women, History, and Theory: The Essays of Joan Kelly.* Chicago: University of Chicago Press, 1984.

Kemp, Martin. *Christ to Coke: How Image Becomes Icon.* Oxford: Oxford University Press, 2012.

Kemp, Martin, ed. *Leonardo on Painting.* New Haven: Yale University Press, 2001.

Kemp, Martin, and Giuseppe Pallanti. *Mona Lisa: The People and the Painting.* Oxford: Oxford University Press, 2017.

King, Ross. *Leonardo and the Last Supper.* New York: Bloomsbury, 2012.

Leader, Darian. *Stealing the Mona Lisa: What Art Stops Us from Seeing.* New York: Counterpoint, 2002.

Livingstone, Margaret. *Vision and Art: The Biology of Seeing.* New York: Abrams, 2014.

Macintyre, Ben. *The Napoleon of Crime: The Life and Times of Adam Worth, Master Thief.* New York: Farrar Straus & Giroux, 1997.

McMullen, Roy. *Mona Lisa: The Picture and the Myth.* New York: Houghton Mifflin, 1975.

Merriman, John. *Ballad of the Anarchist Bandits: The Crime Spree that Gripped Belle Époque Paris.* New York: Bold Type Books, 2017.

Migiel, Marilyn, and Juliana Schiesari, eds. *Refiguring Woman: Perspectives on Gender and the Italian Renaissance.* Ithaca, NY: Cornell University Press, 1991.

Miller, Arthur I. *Einstein, Picasso: Space, Time and the Beauty That Causes Havoc.* New York: Basic Books, 2002.

Nesbit, Molly. "The Rat's Ass." *October* 56 (1991): 6.

Nethersole, Scott. *Art and Violence in Early Renaissance Florence.* New Haven: Yale University Press, 2018.

Nicholl, Charles. *Leonardo da Vinci: Flights of the Mind.* New York: Viking, 2004.

Nici, John B. *Famous Works of Art and How They Got That Way.* Lanham, MD: Rowman & Littlefield, 2017.

Olivier, Fernande. *Picasso and His Friends.* New York: Appleton-Century, 1965.

Pater, Walter. *Studies in the History of the Renaissance.* New York: Oxford University Press, 2010.

Reit, Seymour. *The Day They Stole the Mona Lisa.* New York: Summit Books, 1981.

Rhodes, Henry T .F. *Alphonse Bertillon, Father of Scientific Detection.* New York: Greenwood Press, 1968.

Richardson, John. *A Life of Picasso: The Cubist Rebel, 1907–1916.* New York: Knopf, 2007.

Richardson, John. *A Life of Picasso: The Triumphant Years, 1917–1932.* New York: Knopf, 2010.

Sassoon, Donald. *Becoming Mona Lisa: The Making of a Global Icon.* New York: Harcourt, 2001.

Scotti, R. A. *Vanished Smile: The Mysterious Theft of Mona Lisa.*
New York: Knopf, 2009.

Starr, Douglass. *The Killer of Little Shepherds: A True Crime Story
and the Birth of Forensic Science.* New York: Knopf, 2010.

Steegmuller, Francis. *Apollinaire: Poet Among the Painters.* New York:
Farrar, Straus, 1963.

Turner, A. Richard. *Inventing Leonardo.* New York: Knopf, 1993.

White, Michael. *Leonardo: The First Scientist.* New York: St.
Martin's Griffin, 2000.

THE THEFT OF THE *MONA LISA*

Details of the theft are taken from Esterow, *The Art Stealers;* Hoobler
and Hoobler, *The Crimes of Paris;* McMullen, *Mona Lisa;* Reit,
The Day They Stole the Mona Lisa; Scotti, *Vanished Smile.*

It was a labyrinth: For the mythic history of the Louvre, see
Gardner, *The Louvre.*

THE LUDICROUS FAME OF THE *MONA LISA*

A year before the theft, in a spooky coincidence: Scotti, *Vanished
Smile,* 56.

MONDAY MORNING

"This painting," he said, pointing to the *Mona Lisa:* Esterow,
The Art Stealers, 103.

"They have taken it away": Esterow, *The Art Stealers,* 104.

BRIGADIER PAUPARDIN HAS A VERY BAD DAY

Being photographed, I suppose: Scotti, *Vanished Smile,* 19.

It was a single pane of glass: Scotti, *Vanished Smile,* 18.

The day is wasted: Scotti, *Vanished Smile,* 20.

La Joconde, *c'est partie!:* Scotti, *Vanished Smile,* 21.

LOUIS LÉPINE IS ON THE CASE

He once decreed: Hoobler and Hoobler, *The Crimes of Paris,* 134.

"La Joconde is gone": Scotti, *Vanished Smile,* 25.

UNIMAGINABLE

INIMAGINABLE: Hoobler and Hoobler, *The Crimes of Paris,* 43.

THE *MONA LISA* HAS DISAPPEARED FROM THE LOUVRE: Nici, *Famous Works of Art,* 94.

"What audacious criminal": Hoobler and Hoobler, *The Crimes of Paris,* 46.

On a single day, L'Illustration: Freundschuh, "Crime Stories in the Historical Urban Landscape," 275.

It ran a photo of Notre-Dame: Scotti, *Vanished Smile,* 56.

A physicist named Albert Einstein: The uncanny connection between Einstein and Picasso is outlined in Miller, *Einstein, Picasso.*

VINCI, APRIL 15, 1452

The parents are: A long mysterious matter finally settled in Kemp and Pallanti, *Mona Lisa: The People and the Painting.*

FLORENCE, 1466

Around this same time, Ser Piero: Nicholl, *Leonardo da Vinci,* 105–107.

Get the measurement: Isaacson, *Leonardo da Vinci,* 5.

Observe the goose's foot: Isaacson, *Leonardo da Vinci,* 5.

Observe the curling motion: Nicholl, *Leonardo da Vinci,* 450.

Get the master of arithmetic: Isaacson, *Leonardo da Vinci,* 5.

Describe what sneezing is: Nicholl, *Leonardo da Vinci,* 7.

Inflate the lungs of a pig: Isaacson, *Leonardo da Vinci,* 6.

Anatomize the bat: Nicholl, *Leonardo da Vinci,* 431.

By what means they walk on ice: Isaacson, *Leonardo da Vinci,* 5.

The moon is dense: Nicholl, *Leonardo da Vinci,* 6.

When Leonardo tests out a new quill: Nicholl, *Leonardo da Vinci,* 7.

He describes himself: Nicholl, *Leonardo da Vinci,* 54.

Describe the tongue of a woodpecker: Isaacson, *Leonardo da Vinci,*
525.

FLORENCE, 1479

Decades later, the great Michelangelo: Nicholl, *Leonardo da Vinci,*
379.

Michelangelo is a jerk: For more on the Leonardo–Michelangelo
rivalry, see Jones, *The Lost Battles.*

A FEW VERY SENSIBLE THEORIES

"Feeling here about the affair": Scotti, *Vanished Smile,* 44.

One clairvoyant said the painting: Scotti, *Vanished Smile,* 48.

According to Pilu: Leader, *Stealing the Mona Lisa,* 171.

"Are we dealing with a real theft": Esterow, *The Art Stealers,* 106.

"This surpasses the imagination": Esterow, *The Art Stealers,* 107.

It was around this time: Esterow, *The Art Stealers,* 121.

THE LOUVRE IS A CRIME SCENE

But this new century was the dawn: For more on the development of
forensic science, see Starr, *The Killer of Little Shepherds.*

A weird thing happened: For this wonderful idea, I am indebted to Leader, *Stealing the Mona Lisa*.

"I love you": Hoobler and Hoobler, *The Crimes of Paris*, 65.

And second, the theft was planned: Scotti, *Vanished Smile*, 60.

THE MAN WITH THE WRONG NAME

When Bertillon's father registered: Rhodes, *Alphonse Bertillon*, 28–29.

A decade or so before the Mona Lisa theft: All quotes in the Vernet episode are from Goron, *Pearson's Magazine*.

Suspicion quickly focused: For more on the sensational Dreyfus affair, see Harris, *Dreyfus*.

"The proof is there": Hoobler and Hoobler, *The Crimes of Paris*, 167.

IT TAKES A THIEF TO CATCH A THIEF

Is Arsène Lupin Alive?: Hoobler and Hoobler, *The Crimes of Paris*, 68.

"I preferred men": Hoobler and Hoobler, *The Crimes of Paris*, 74.

A vivid example: Hoobler and Hoobler, *The Crimes of Paris*, 137–138.

Locard's motto was: Hoobler and Hoobler, *The Crimes of Paris*, 138.

A BREAK IN THE CASE

Fingerprinting solved both problems: For more on the strange case of Henry Faulds, see Beavan, *Fingerprints*. For more on the complexities of fingerprinting as a method of identification, see Cole, *Suspect Identities*.

FLORENCE, 1481

He makes it all up: Nicholl, *Leonardo da Vinci,* 180–182.

Describe the jaw of crocodile: Isaacson, *Leonardo da Vinci,* 398.

Describe the beginning of a human: Isaacson, *Leonardo da Vinci,* 178–179.

Describe how the clouds are formed: Nicholl, *Leonardo da Vinci,* 7.

"The space between the mouth": Isaacson, *Leonardo da Vinci,* 219.

In a notebook, he writes: Isaacson, *Leonardo da Vinci,* 126.

MILAN, 1493

"Neither Greece nor Rome": Isaacson, *Leonardo da Vinci,* 165.

Leonardo is brokenhearted: Nicholl, *Leonardo da Vinci,* 291–292.

For his next act, Leonardo starts work: For a popular account of *The Last Supper,* see King, *Leonardo and the Last Supper.*

It's described as a "muddle of blots": Nicholl, *Leonardo da Vinci,* 302.

In his notebooks, there's a strange sentence: Nicholl, *Leonardo da Vinci,* 321.

Mirror script is often thought: Isaacson, *Leonardo da Vinci,* 32.

"Sell what you cannot": Nicholl, *Leonardo da Vinci,* 322.

THE LOUVRE REOPENS

It even attracted the young, depressive Franz Kafka: For more on Kafka and the silent short, see Belting, *The Invisible Masterpiece.*

"The *Mona Lisa* was so beautiful": Scotti, *Vanished Smile,* 82.

"There is not even one guard": Esterow, *The Art Stealers,* 111.

"In the Interest of Art": Hoobler and Hoobler, *The Crimes of Paris,* 48.

A week after the theft, the *Mona Lisa* herself: Hoobler and Hoobler, *The Crimes of Paris,* 44.

"The entire world sat back aghast": Scotti, *Vanished Smile,* 29.

"The eyes of the world": "*Mona Lisa,*" *Canadian Century,* September 9, 1911.

"Energetic searchings continue": "Theft of a Picture," *Queensland Times,* August 29, 1911.

"There appears to be much mystery": "Priceless Picture Stolen," *Bath Chronicle and Weekly Gazette,* August 24, 1911.

THE INGENIOUS THIEF

We can guess what Lépine was thinking: Hoobler and Hoobler, *The Crimes of Paris,* 57.

There were classes: Hoobler and Hoobler, *The Crimes of Paris,* 57.

Adam Worth was a celebrity: For the very colorful life of Adam Worth, see Macintyre, *The Napoleon of Crime.*

"He is the organizer of half that is evil": Macintyre, *The Napoleon of Crime,* 223.

"All that I ever require": Hoobler and Hoobler, *The Crimes of Paris,* 56.

FLORENCE, 1494

This money is called a dowry: For more on dowries in Renaissance Italy, see Hales, *Mona Lisa,* 66–67 and 94–95.

So many deaths: Nethersole, *Art and Violence in Early Renaissance Florence,* 39. For more on the brutality of the scene and how it was later represented, see Nethersole, "Visualizing Violence: The Pazzi Conspiracy."

"For love of war": Hales, *Mona Lisa,* 66.

THE RICH AMERICAN

"It is generally conceded": Scotti, *Vanished Smile*, 61.

"The belief is very general": Scotti, *Vanished Smile*, 51.

"I have not been offered": Scotti, *Vanished Smile*, 54.

DR. NO (PART 1)

"Query not that I have the Goya": Hirsch, *The Duke of Wellington, Kidnapped!*, 52.

"Be very careful with this": Hirsch, *The Duke of Wellington, Kidnapped!*, 94.

"The guards were having a cup of tea": Hirsch, *The Duke of Wellington, Kidnapped!*, 114.

"There will appear gigantic figures": Nicholl, *Leonardo da Vinci*, 2.

WILL YOU BUY IT?

"Europe has a great deal of art": Houpt, *Museum of the Missing*, 27.

"I must see you alone": All quotes in this scene are from Duveen, *Art Treasures and Intrigue*, 316–317.

FLORENCE, 1495

"O do not be": Hales, *Mona Lisa*, 126.

She is like nearly every other woman: The landmark article on this subject is Kelly, "Did Women Have a Renaissance?" (She answered her own question in the negative.)

This is a (partial) list: Hales, *Mona Lisa*, 88–89.

"In Florence, women are more enclosed": Migiel and Schiesari, *Refiguring Woman*, 65.

FLORENCE, 1500

"Leonardo's life is extremely irregular": Nicholl, *Leonardo da Vinci,*
336–337.

The friar apologizes: Nicholl, *Leonardo da Vinci,* 336–337.

WHY THIS PAINTING?

We can look past its fame: For a skimming of the depths of
the *Mona Lisa,* see Kemp and Pallanti, *Mona Lisa: The People
and the Painting,* 175–195; and Sassoon, *Becoming Mona
Lisa,* 31–38.

He wrote that women should be painted: Kemp, *Leonardo on
Painting,* 147.

This is the spooky way: For the science of this phenomenon, see
Livingstone, *Vision and Art,* 71–73.

A STATUE STOLEN FROM THE LOUVRE

A Thief Brings Us: Esterow, *The Art Stealers,* 123.

It was in March, 1907: Esterow, *The Art Stealers,* 124–126.

But there is no story sadder: For more of the endlessly quotable
Apollinaire, see Steegmuller, *Apollinaire.*

his eyebrows were like commas: For this detail, now an essential
part of any Apollinaire description, I am indebted to Fernande
Olivier, in *Picasso and His Friends,* 36.

"Guillaume was extraordinarily brilliant": Scotti, *Vanished Smile,*
96–97.

We were like mountain climbers: Richardson, *A Life of Picasso:
The Cubist Rebel, 1907–1916,* 59.

TWO STATUES AND A PISTOL

"Can I bring you anything you need?": Steegmuller, *Apollinaire*, 190.

The other half he discovered: For more on Picasso and the influence of the Trocadéro, see Cohen, *The "Black Art" Renaissance*, 55–92.

"I understood why I was a painter": Richardson, *A Life of Picasso: The Cubist Rebel, 1907–1916*, 24.

In the history of modern art: For more on the seemingly inexhaustible subject of *Les Demoiselles d'Avignon*, see Green, *Picasso's Les Demoiselles d'Avignon;* and Richardson, *A Life of Picasso: The Cubist Rebel, 1907–1916*, 24–45.

"If you look at the ears": Charney, *Art and Crime*, 59.

DR. NO (PART 2)

He was said to stalk: Charney, *Art and Crime*, 58.

"They thought they were being followed": Olivier, *Picasso and His Friends*, 147.

"I hope with all my heart": Esterow, *The Art Stealers*, 131.

THE ENEMY WITHIN

"We are on the trail": Esterow, *The Art Stealers*, 132.

"I found myself suddenly stared at": Scotti, *Vanished Smile*, 105.

"I have never seen him before": Scotti, *Vanished Smile*, 106.

THE MAN WHO HAD STOLEN THE *MONA LISA*

"I had an impression of death": Esterow, *The Art Stealers*, 136.

"Guillaume Apollinaire abruptly became famous": Esterow, *The Art Stealers*, 122.

ROME, 1513

"Alas, this man will never do anything": Nicholl, *Leonardo da Vinci*, 466.

In order to outline all the veins: Nicholl, *Leonardo da Vinci*, 422.

"The pope has found out": Isaacson, *Leonardo da Vinci*, 461.

FRANCE, 1516

Francis calls Leonardo: Hales, *Mona Lisa*, 209.

He later says: Nicholl, *Leonardo da Vinci*, 486–487.

PARIS, 1850

Standing before this portrait: Kemp and Pallanti, *Mona Lisa*, 128.

Above all, Gautier is enthralled: Kemp and Pallanti, *Mona Lisa*, 128.

But he's also disturbed: Sassoon, *Becoming Mona Lisa*, 111.

Gautier makes the Mona Lisa: For the complete story of how the
Mona Lisa became mysterious, see Sassoon, *Becoming Mona Lisa*,
91–132.

"Beware, La Gioconda is a dangerous picture": Hales, *Mona Lisa*, 236.

"For years I have grappled desperately": Hales, *Mona Lisa*, 235.

The English critic Walter Pater: Sassoon, *Becoming Mona Lisa*, 134–135.

The Irish writer Oscar Wilde: Sassoon, *Becoming Mona Lisa*, 146–147.

Before they came along: Boas, "The Mona Lisa in the History of
Taste," 215.

THERE IS NO GROUND TO HOPE

The Bonnot Gang was a group of anarchists: For more on turn-
of-the-century French anarchism and the Bonnot gang, see
Merriman, *Ballad of the Anarchist Bandits*.

The official investigation was closed: Scotti, *Vanished Smile*, 154.

LEONARD

Geri was about to toss the letter: Esterow, *The Art Stealers*, 145.

A MANGLED HAT, A MANDOLIN

Geri later made a list: Esterow, *The Art Stealers*, 147.

"To our astonished eyes": Esterow, *The Art Stealers*, 147.

A HOUSEPAINTER

No, the curator told the caller: Esterow, *The Art Stealers*, 149.

"I only wish that the French": Scotti, *Vanished Smile*, 171.

"*La Gioconda ha trovato*": Scotti, *Vanished Smile*, 164.

"I would be unworthy of Italy": Scotti, *Vanished Smile*, 169.

"I have rendered outstanding service to Italy": Hoobler and Hoobler,
  The Crimes of Paris, 259.

NO WORD SPOKEN BUT GIOCONDA

"No word is spoken but 'Gioconda'": Esterow, *The Art Stealers*,
  157.

"Although the masterpiece is dear": Scotti, *Vanished Smile*, 172.

"Oh, it is she, it is she": Esterow, *The Art Stealers*, 157.

A NOBLE MISTAKE

"I would sooner have gone around": Duveen, *Art Treasures and
  Intrigue*, 317.

Perugia claimed he'd just wanted "advice": Esterow, *The Art Stealers*,
  165.

Besides, he didn't want: Esterow, *The Art Stealers*, 150.

"I do not believe Perugia's story": Scotti, *Vanished Smile*, 166.

Meanwhile, the Louvre's fired director: Scotti, *Vanished Smile*, 166.

THE MARQUIS

It told the tale: Decker, "Why and How the Mona Lisa Was Stolen,"
15–16, 89–92

He had a head of "leonine" white hair: Decker, "Why and How the
Mona Lisa Was Stolen," 14.

It was, Valfierno said, "the most magnificent single theft": Decker,
"Why and How the Mona Lisa Was Stolen," 91.

LAST WORDS

"The most influential and prolific painter": Bernard Valery, "Death
Stills Picasso's Brush at 91," *New York Daily News,* April 9, 1973.

"The titan of 20th century art": "Picasso Is Dead in France at 91,"
The New York Times, April 9, 1973.

"When the judge asked me": Scotti, *Vanished Smile,* 117.

"A few days ago, I was sitting": Richardson, *A Life of Picasso: The
Cubist Rebel, 1907–1916,* 205.

THE SOUP

"Et cetera," he writes: Nicholl, *Leonardo da Vinci,* 1.

EPILOGUE

When it visited the Soviet Union: Hales, *Mona Lisa,* 244.

In New York, a visitor stared in wonder: Leader, *Stealing the Mona
Lisa,* 5.

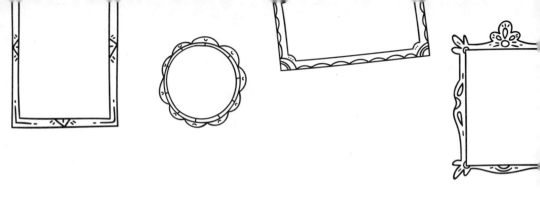

INDEX